Th
CEMI
RAILWAYS
OF KENT

by
B.D. Stoyel
R.W. Kidner

THE OAKWOOD PRESS

© Oakwood Press 1990

ISBN 0 85361 370 2

First Edition 1973

Second Enlarged Edition 1990

Typeset by Gem Publishing Company, Brightwell, Wallingford, Oxfordshire.

Printed by Alpha Print, Witney, Oxfordshire.

All rights reserved. No part of this book may be reproduced or transmitted in any form or by any means, electronic or mechanical, including photo-copying, recording or by any information storage and retrieval system, without permission from the Publisher in writing.

At the Burham Works, the Hudswell Clarke engine *Killarney* propels empty wagons from the loop into the bottom pit; it is just entering the tunnel over which ran a spur to the top pit; September 1937.   *R.W. Kidner*

Title page: Aylesford near Burham Works.   *R.W. Kidner*

Published by
The OAKWOOD PRESS
P.O.Box 122, Headington, Oxford.

Contents

3

The Stone Court Chalk Co. Falcon engine *Quarrier* with a loaded train from the pits arriving at the point where lines from the Whiting works, the Atlas Stone Co. and Kent Works all met, in September 1933.

R.W. Kidner

Foreword

During the 16 years since this book was first published, the process of rationalisation of Kent cement works, which had begun before it was written has now been completed. The works and railways are not being used, as was then the case; now they are mostly not even there, and modern earth-moving equipment soon removed all traces. However, along with this process, there has been a great increase in interest in industrial railways and industrial archaeology generally. Thus the call for the reissue of this book, and the opportunity has been taken to include further information which has come in from readers and researchers.

The authors wish to give heartfelt thanks to these correspondents, and especially to Messrs John Fletcher, C. Down, and Tom Burnham, who have supplied much of the new material.

Thanks also to those whose personal reminiscences are included in the Appendices; the recollections of little engines in white pits stayed powerfully with them, from the days of youth when the sun always shone.

1990 Edition   *B.D. Stoyel*
                                                                  R.W. Kidner

Introduction

Anyone who has travelled beside the Thames in the Dartford–Gravesend area or beside the Medway between Rochester and Maidstone must surely have been impressed by the huge chalk quarries in the hills which fringe these two rivers, mostly now long worked-out and overgrown in places with vegetation. If the traveller is old enough to remember these same valleys forty or more years ago he will probably call to mind scenes of great activity, for here was the real centre of the English cement industry. What is reputed to be the first kiln for the production of Portland cement, known as Aspdin's kiln, is still preserved at Northfleet as a monument to the industry. The manufacture of cement is indeed still centred around this area, but through a long period of rationalisation the industry has become concentrated in a few large works, leaving numerous other superseded works to fall gradually into decay. The scenes of activity during this period were not confined to the cement works themselves. The principal raw material is, of course, chalk but clay is needed; the works were sited here because of the abundant supplies which were available, but also because the proximity of the Thames or the Medway offered a ready means of transport. At its origin the cement works was usually situated close to both of these necessities, i.e. a potential chalk quarry and a suitable place for a river wharf, and almost invariably a railway was constructed to link the factory with both. As the chalk near to the works became exhausted, further quarries had to be opened up, often connected by tunnels through ground which could not be dug for chalk owing to the presence of roads or buildings on the surface, until eventually the railway might have to run for a considerable distance to serve the latest quarry to be opened up. As moreover the exact spot, and also the level, of the current excavation was constantly changing, so the railway tracks had to alter their course in order to follow suit.

Initially there were a large number of small independent companies, each as a rule operating only one cement works. At this period, too, little use was made of the main line railway for transporting the finished product and the great bulk of the cement was despatched from the river wharf, mainly in picturesque and typical Thames sailing barges. In view of the absence of railway connections, the cement lines would not usually be constructed to the standard gauge, and to this fact can be attributed the astonishing variety of narrow gauges that were to be found. Equally astonishing was the variety of locomotives and rolling stock, and in these days of enthusiasm for all types of antiquated machinery there must be many who greatly regret that they were not born early enough to witness these scenes.

At the larger works there would be a fairly constant succession of trains of chalk wagons running to and from the quarries. When seen from the top of one of the chalk cliffs created by the excavations over a long period, these could be a most impressive sight; even more so if one was privileged to be down in the pit bottom, marvelling that the lurching tip-wagons kept to the track, and that the engine did not break an axle on the villainous track-joints. To a lesser extent there would be similar activity on the line or lines leading to the wharf, but usually this was only a short distance.

The authors first became acquainted with this fascinating area towards the end of 1929 and it immediately became a favourite objective for a Saturday or holiday-time excursion. At that time, to show an interest in industrial locomotives was regarded as an extreme eccentricity, even by the quite numerous band of confirmed railway enthusiasts, and no books were available to list and describe what could be found in this field up and down the country. There was therefore a very strong element of adventure and exploration, and for quite a long time nearly every visit to the cement-producing area would bring to light some fresh locomotive not previously encountered.

When the district had been thoroughly searched and it was thought that there were no further locomotives left to discover, it was natural that one's thoughts began to turn to the earlier locomotives that had already disappeared before there had been an opportunity to see them. The existing drivers then proved a most fruitful source of information regarding the past, and it was soon realised that here was a class of men who had remarkably retentive and precise memories so far as locomotives and dates were concerned. It is probable that the first thoughts of recording the history of the cement works railways arose from a desire to put on permanent record the recollections of this astonishing breed of men.

Both authors must also admit to being unashamedly steam enthusiasts and interest in other forms of motive power is very slight. It should therefore be emphasised that this book is intended to cover the age of steam, and that diesel, petrol or electric locomotives have received little or no mention. Although some of these railways commenced with horse haulage, the steam locomotive has undoubtedly been both the mainstay and the centre of attraction of the cement lines, and the demise of steam has not long preceded the demise of the railways themselves.

The number of different sources from which information has been gathered makes it very difficult to make adequate acknowledgment of the help given by numerous people. So many of them must remain anonymous for the simple reason that their names were never known to the writers. The men on the spot were simply asked for information and almost invariably it was very readily given. Special mention must be made, however, of Mr D.R. Lamb, the Engineer at the Swanscombe Works, and of Mr S.B. Fletcher of Maidstone, who had been closely concerned in his younger days with Lee's works at Halling. Both these gentlemen have been most helpful and almost alone amongst those connected with the cement industry they have provided information in writing instead of orally.

It would be quite wrong to suggest that the authors have been personally responsible for collecting even the greater part of the locomotive details recorded in this little work. It has really been a joint effort on the part of a large number of steam enthusiasts. Here again it is impossible to acknowledge their help individually in every case, but the majority of them have been fellow-members of the Industrial Locomotive Society. Most of all Derek Stoyel would like to record his appreciation of the great help given by the late George Alliez, his companion on many a cement works visit, official or more often unofficial, and a prolific and skilful photographer as well as an accomplished historian of industrial locomotives. Special acknowledgment should also be made to Messrs T. Burnham, J.S. Brownlie, C.G. Down, A. Duke, J. Faithfull, W.J. Fletcher, R.T. Russell and R.F. Weeden, R. Burchett, C. Fleetney, A.H. Lambert, D. Gould, B. Henderson, and to all who have given permission for their photographs to be reproduced.

Note on the Plans

By the nature of the work, the tracks of the cement railway were constantly moving; almost the only things which did not change were the tunnels. In the town areas, such as Northfleet itself, the tracks moved from one small pit to another as they became worked out, leaving the streets and lanes more or less on stilts, and the routes can be clearly seen even today. When the lines stretched out into the open country, they cut great open-cast swathes into the chalk deposits, often working on several levels simultaneously, and after the rails were shifted they left no trace.

The tracks shown in pits are therefore only a rough indication; in the same way, plant and buildings changed and no attempt has been made to show these in detail. Plans cannot of course show differences in level. In general, chalk pits were cut through to the bottom and then worked, usually on more than one level, by steam excavators working upwards (i.e. bringing the chalk down to the railway). Clay-pits, on the other hand, were usually worked by a grab or drag-line above the pit, pulling the clay upwards. Often the clay-pits were on the riverside, as were the works, and the short distance enabled the railway in some cases to be replaced by belt conveyors.

National Grid References

As far as possible the Grid References quoted with the section headings are intended to show location of the locomotive shed, although in a few cases where its position is not known, it has been assumed to be at the main works.

All the railways covered by this book are within the 100 km square TQ and for reasons of simplicity this prefix has been omitted from the Grid References.

Cement-Producing Companies

With the solitary exception of the Rugby Portland Cement Co.'s plant at Halling, all the cement works in Kent have latterly been owned by Associated Portland Cement Manufacturers Ltd (usually abbreviated as APCM), including their associated company British Portland Cement Manufacturers Ltd set up in 1910 (officially from 1st January, 1911). The last works in Kent to be acquired by this group was Alpha Cement Ltd, with a works at Cliffe, which was taken over in 1949.

The APCM was formed in 1900 by an amalgamation of the great majority of the Kent cement manufacturers, as well as a number elsewhere. Until 1919 their title was Associated Portland Cement Manufacturers (1900) Ltd. It became Blue Circle Industries plc in 1978.

While on the subject of ownership, it is worth mentioning that although most companies owned all four elements — chalk, claypit, railway and works — it was not always the case. 'Buying in' chalk and clay was not uncommon, and in some cases the railway and wharfage were operated by a different company from that running the cement-producing works.

Rail Gauges

Seven different gauges were used when laying the early cement lines; at the time nobody foresaw the need to connect with the standard gauge railways, since water transport was traditional on the Thames and Medway; nor did it occur that the time might come when works were amalgamated. The reason for the choice of any particular gauge cannot now be fathomed; the most likely one would be the existence of an early horse tramway laid by a local ironworks to no particular gauge, but followed when expanding into steam. Another might be a maker's offer of rolling stock, perhaps 'frustrated exports' at a low price. At a later stage, almost all works did have their sidings from the SE&CR, also light tramways for temporary works (not included in the above seven) so that several works had three gauges in use. From the mid-1920s almost all converted the works and quarry lines to standard gauge, which enabled the Group to move engines around with ease, and also made it easier to buy in second-hand locomotives.

Liveries

The APCM livery was yellow with a blue circle, and this was applied to all road vehicles and to the Johnsons' electric transporters and the Kent Works carriage. The engines however were painted in various shades of green, with a few exceptions: three of the Northfleet Deepwater Wharf engines were red, and two at Broom Bank were blue with yellow lining (possibly applied at Wouldham Hall), and in the last years one or two engines appeared in yellow. Except at Bevan's after 1925, identification was by name; these were normally on cast plates but there were exceptions; at Stone Court only W H Liversidge carried a plate, the others being painted. Names were not changed on transfer; this had one interesting result: Tolhurst at Northfleet had named all its engines after animals, so that after this works was closed, and transfers made, three other works had an engine named after an animal. Similarly, three engines named after letters of the Greek alphabet could be found, having crossed over from Essex. Naming fell out of fashion, and at Swanscombe after relaying, only numbers were carried; latterly at Kent Works engines carried both names and numbers.

Hustler was a narrow gauge engine built by the Kilmarnock Engine Co. for Whites Works, Swanscombe in 1920; as with all the others at this works, the wheels had outside flanges.   Locomotive Publishing Co.

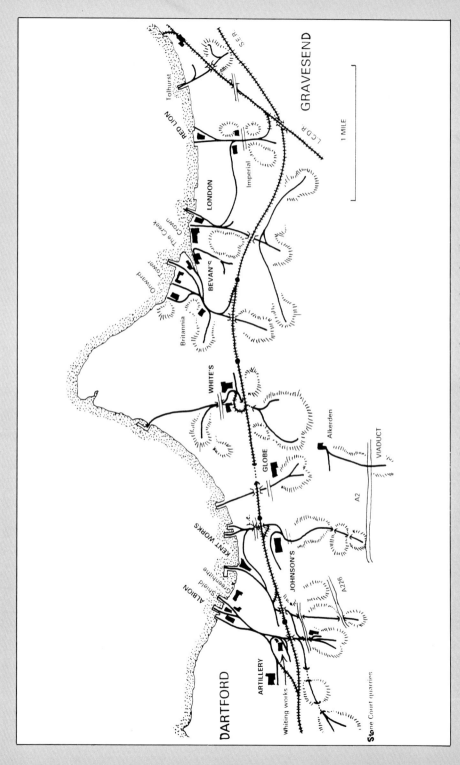

Schematic map showing the location of the works situated on the Thames Estuary.

Part One

Thames Estuary: West to East

DARTFORD CEMENT WORKS LTD
542748

At Dartford a line ran from a pit opposite the present railway carriage sidings, to a small works opened about 1891 and then down to a wharf on Dartford Creek. It seems probable that this line was horse-worked, and it closed down in 1911, after takeover by BPCM. However it was still marked as a cement works on the 1931 6 in. OS map, and a branch from the tramway had been built 500 yds southwards into the Burroughs Wellcome chemical factory.

ARTILLERY & ALBION CEMENT CO. LTD, STONE COURT
567752 (Artillery) 574756 (Albion)

A group of cement works was built on the Stone Court estate east of Dartford. The Albion, on the river front, was set up by William Fry about 1873, and sold in 1890 by Henry Jones to J.G. Collier, who formed the Albion Cement Co. Ltd in 1896. Next to it on the east was the Shield Works, started by Messrs Wilders & Cary around 1890. East again was the Greenhithe Works, established by the Gillingham Portland Cement Co. Ltd in 1889, and acquired by J.B. White in 1893. A short distance to the south-west was the Artillery Works, established by F.E. Rosher about 1880; in 1903 this was amalgamated with Albion as the Artillery & Albion Cement Co. Ltd; however at this time the former was marked on maps as 'disused'. Wilders & Cary joined APCM in 1900; Artillery & Albion joined BPCM in 1910. All except possibly Greenhithe were closed by 1913, but a whiting works north of Stone Court Crossing continued in use. The works obtained chalk at first from small pits north of the South Eastern Railway, but from 1885 it was supplied by the Stone Court Chalk Land & Pier Co. (*see below*).

The locomotives were as follows:

Name	Wheel arr.	Maker & Maker's No.	Date Built	Cylinders	Wheel Diameter
Stonecourt	0−4−0ST			outs. cyls	
Artillery	0−4−0ST	Falcon, 240	1896	outs. cyls	
Albion	0−4−0ST	Peckett, 915	1901	outs. cyls 10″ × 14″	2′ 6½″

No details of *Stonecourt* are available, but it is understood to have been already there when *Artillery* arrived and to have been sold in about 1915. *Albion* was supplied new. Both *Artillery* and *Albion* were transferred by the APCM to Hilton's Works at Halling when the works at Stone were closed.

STONE COURT CHALK, LAND & PIER CO. LTD
569750

This was not a cement-producing concern, but worked closely with several cement works and was later part of APCM. The Stone Court Chalk,

11

Land and Pier Co. Ltd as it was first called, took over, in about 1885, a pier and tramway on Stone Marsh which had been set up some twelve years earlier. Adjacent to the pier were the Albion, Shield, and Greenhithe Cement Works, and the Artillery Cement Works was a little way inland to the south-west. All were served by a railway of standard gauge, which also ran south, under the SER and Cotton Lane, to a chalk pit. Just north of the tunnel under the SER there was a whiting works. In 1908 the branch line to the Artillery Works was extended to an exchange siding with the SER North Kent Line.

When the Kent Works was built to the east, a cutting was made parallel to the SER and south of it, with a connection to the Stone Court line just north of Cotton Lane tunnel, so that material could be worked from the pit to the new works. At about the same time, a further cutting was made south of the SER to enable Stone Court trains to run to new pits to the west. Since this line had to tunnel under Cotton Lane twice and also under Moody's Lane, at great depth, there were in effect three pits in line. Some chalk from here went to Kent Works; however the layout at Cotton Lane tunnel was such that these trains had to run into the whiting works, reverse into the pit, and then reverse out again to hand the train over to a Kent Works engine. Some time before the last War this was altered so that trains could run straight through. However, a company called the Atlas Stone Company had established itself by 1928 at the bottom of the original pit, being served by Stone Court trains with materials. In 1935 Stone Court Ballast Co. was working gravel pits near the river shore, using high-sided wagons, unlike the small chalk tippers. Much of this went to Atlas Stone, and in the latter years when a square crossing had been laid at Cotton Lane tunnel, this meant that trains from the gravel pits to Atlas Stone crossed the path of chalk trains from the pits to Kent Works, and it is said that 'traffic lights' were installed to control the crossing.

Stone Court chalk operations were abandoned in 1949, and the engines either scrapped or transferred, except for one which was sold to Atlas Stone to continue gravel traffic. Kent Works continued to win chalk from the west pits until 1956.

The company, which had changed its name to Stone Court Ballast Co. Ltd, in 1929, remained in existence and its assets were transferred in 1974 to APCM, and later to Blue Circle Investments Ltd in 1975. The shape of things in this area has been transformed by the Dartford Tunnel, the power station, and other developments.

Stone Court Locomotives:

Adamant	0–4–0ST	Manning Wardle, 649	1877	outs. cyls 8″ × 14″	2′ 8″
Bulldog	0–4–0ST	Manning Wardle, 13	1860	outs. cyls 8″ × 14″	
Sundridge	0–4–0ST	Hughes		outs. cyls 11″ × ?	
James Godwin	0–4–0ST	Shanks	1870	outs. cyls 10″ × 20″	3′ 1″
Quarrier	0–4–0ST	Falcon, 203	1891	outs. cyls 11″ × 18″	3′ 0″
Longreach	0–4–0ST	Falcon, 236	1896	outs. cyls 11″ × 18″	3′ 0″
Flintfield	0–4–0ST	Brush, 277	1898	outs. cyls 12″ × 20″	3′ 0″
W.H. Liversidge	0–4–0ST	Brush, 286	1899	outs. cyls 11″ × 18″	3′ 0″
Lion	0–4–0ST	Falcon, 205	1891	outs. cyls 11″ × 18″	3′ 0″
Iota	0–4–0T	Falcon, 211	1892	outs. cyls 11″ × 18″	3′ 0″

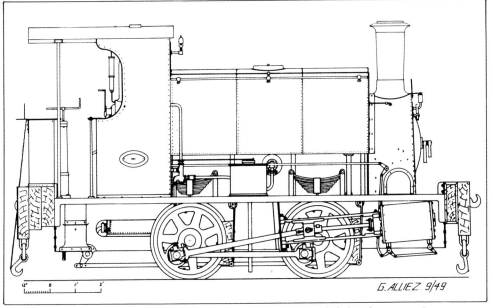

A scaled side-elevation of the type of 0–4–0ST provided for the Stone Court Company by the Falcon Engine Co. Ltd of Loughborough; some bore plates of the Brush Electrical Engineering Co. which took the works over.

The Stone Court Ballast Co. Ltd Falcon engine *Longreach* at the Stone works on 10th October, 1946.   *B.D. Stoyel*

Of the above, *Sundridge, Quarrier, Longreach, Flintfield* and *W.H. Liversidge* were supplied new. There is some suggestion that *Sundridge* was a vertical-boilered locomotive which was scrapped just before the turn of the century, but no confirmation has been found for this. *Adamant* had previously belonged to the Britannia London Portland Cement Co. at Seacombe, Birkenhead. *James Godwin* was originally built for the Southampton Dock Co. but came to Stone from the London & St Katherine Dock Co. (their No. 16) some time before 1896. *Bulldog* and *Lion* came from the APCM's Tolhurst Works at Northfleet and *Iota* from their Gibb's Works at West Thurrock in about 1925. *Iota* was a side-tank with dropped footplate and low vertical clearance.

Locomotive *Adamant* was said to have been scrapped in 1918 and *Bulldog* at an unknown date. *Quarrier, Longreach* and *W.H. Liversidge* were scrapped in 1949 after the railway had been abandoned. *Flintfield* was lent to the APCM Works at Stone in 1947–1948 and was then sold to the Atlas Stone Co. Ltd for use on their adjoining premises. There is some suggestion that *James Godwin* was sold to a firm at Portland. *Lion* was transferred in 1946 to the APCM's Swanscombe Works and was sold in 1948 to the Atlas Stone Co. Ltd. *Iota* was loaned to Alpha Cement Ltd, West Thurrock, from 1945 until 1946 when it was sold to the BPCM Works at Penarth, in South Wales.

KENT PORTLAND CEMENT CO. LTD, STONE
576751

This works has had a relatively short history as it was not constructed until after World War I. It was built from 1919–22 by the contractors, P. & W. Anderson, for the Kent Portland Cement Co. Ltd, but only a year after its completion the company was acquired by APCM. It is situated on the Thames foreshore about ½ mile north-east of Stone Crossing Halt between the railway (and road) and the river, where there was a jetty. There were extensive store areas and sidings between the main works and the SR exchange siding immediately west of Stone Crossing Halt.

It is probable that chalk was originally taken from the pit south of Cotton Lane; however by 1930 a large pit east of this, south of Elizabeth Street, was being worked (now a sports ground). This was progressively opened out down to London Road, and finally a tunnel under that road reached the southernmost pit.

The method of working a face was to lay a double track approaching it, singling at the actual face. As the engine hauled away the full wagons, the empty train would be propelled under the excavator, thus losing no time. The six-coupled engines could take some 16 wagons, loaded to about 3–4 yards each; though with a split-level face the gradient to the top level was sometimes severe, it was always in favour of the loaded trains.

In 1963 a cutting was built to connect the pit with that of Johnson's Branch; there had always been a certain amount of interchange between the two works by a line along the bank of the river.

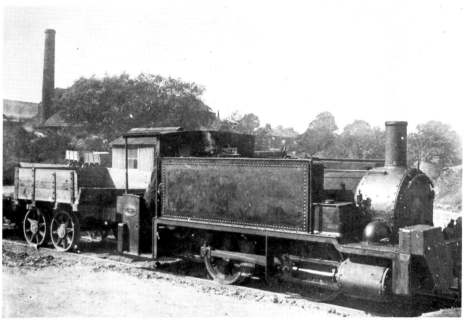

Stone Court Ballast Co. Ltd *Iota*, built by the Falcon Engineering Co. Ltd in 1892, with low vertical clearance, for Gibbs Works at West Thurrock, at the Stone Court Whiting works in September 1933. *R.W. Kidner*

The western extension of the Stone Court line was at low level; this 1932 view shows a train running through the disused first pit, with empty wagons in the loop and at left a line laid for dumping spoil. *R.W. Kidner*

The Kent Works Manning Wardle (1903) engine *Arthur* in 1961, after the locomotive stock was numbered. *G. Alliez*

Kent Works No. 6 in April 1938, with a train of the later outside-bearing wagons. *R.W. Kidner*

Another Manning Wardle engine at Kent Works, *Apex*, built in 1905, being flagged across the road into the works in 1934. *R.W. Kidner*

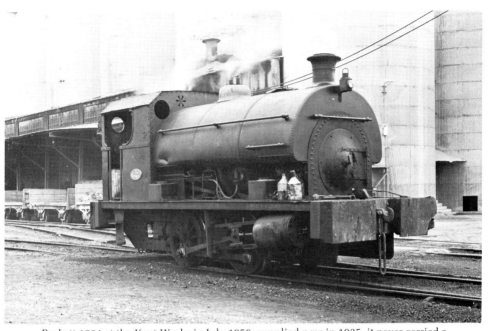

Peckett 1804 at the Kent Works in July 1956; supplied new in 1935, it never carried a name. *G. Alliez*

The Hudswell Clarke engine *Stone*, taken over from the contractors who built the Kent Works in 1922, photographed in August 1935. *G. Alliez*

A Brush engine, *Elephant*, built in 1899 for Tolhurst & Co., at Kent Works in 1947 after rebuilding in the company's works. *Brush E.E. Co. Ltd*

Kent Works No. 2, *Elephant*, hauling a train from the wharf past the offices at the Stone works on 19th April, 1958. *John R.Bonser*

There was a well-built locomotive shed on the western edge of the works area.

The original locomotives were acquired by the Cement Company from Messrs P. & W. Anderson on the completion of their contract in 1922 and details are as follows:

Stone	0−6−0ST	Hudswell Clarke, 298	1888	ins. cyls 12″ × 18″	3′ 0″
Toronto	0−4−0ST	Hudswell Clarke, 571	1900	outs. cyls 10″ × 16″	2′ 9″
Arthur	0−6−0ST	Manning Wardle, 1601	1903	ins. cyls 12″ × 18″	3′ 0″
Apex	0−6−0ST	Manning Wardle, 1657	1905	ins. cyls 12″ × 18″	3′ 0″

These were all of standard contractor's types and were soon reinforced by three locomotives transferred from other works in the APCM combine:

Hilton	0−4−0ST	Peckett, 633	1896	outs. cyls 12″ × 18″	2′ 9″
Elephant	0−4−0ST	Brush, 287	1899	outs. cyls 10″ × 18″	3′ 0″
Clarence	0−4−0ST	Barclay		outs. cyls 10″ × 18″	3′ 3″

The above came respectively from Hilton Works, Halling, Tolhurst Works, Northfleet, and Hilton Works, Grays. *Clarence* originally carried a maker's plate reading 'T.D. Ridley, Middlesborough, No. 13, 1899' but it is believed that it was an older Barclay locomotive rebuilt at that time. The original makers' plates were removed from most of the older locomotives and rather large owners' plates were fitted in their place, showing the makers' numbers but not the makers' names. These plates showed *Elephant*, *Clarence* and *Apex* to have been rebuilt at Kent Works in 1927, 1928 and 1927 respectively, whilst *Stone* had already been rebuilt by the makers in 1909.

The next additions to the locomotive stock were supplied new and they did not carry names:

	0−4−0ST	Peckett, 1804	1935	outs. cyls 14″ × 22″	3′ 2½″
	0−4−0ST	Robt. Stephenson, 7336 & Hawthorn	1947	outs. cyls 16″ × 24″	3′ 8″

After the war a further locomotive was acquired from the Woolwich Arsenal:

	0−4−0ST	Peckett, 1985	1940	outs. cyls 14″ × 20″

Slight alterations had to be made to these locomotives after arrival to enable them to run in tunnels, the chief modification being to the cab roofs.

Stone and *Toronto* were scrapped in 1950, and in 1953 running numbers were allotted to the remaining locomotives as follows:

No. 1	*Clarence*	No. 2	*Elephant*	No. 3	*Arthur*
No. 4	*Apex*	No. 5	*Hilton*	No. 6	Peckett 1804
No. 7	Peckett 1985	No. 8	R.S.H. 7336		

No. 2 at Northfleet Works was subsequently transferred to Stone, its particulars being:

No. 9	0−4−0ST	Peckett, 1702	1926	outs. cyls 14″ × 22″	3′ 2½″

Opposite: This map reproduced from the 1934 edition of the 25" O.S. shows top left, the line to the old Artillery Works (removed) and below that the exchange siding with the SE&CR North Kent Line; on the right of that, the Stone Court Whiting Works, and the line up to the wharf, where the Albion, Shield, and Greenhithe Works once stood. South of the railway are the new Stone Court pits on the left, the old one, centre, and the new Kent Works pit, right. The Kent Works exchange siding is behind Stone Crossing Halt. Note that the junction south of Cotton Lane has been relaid for through running from the Stone Court pits to Kent Works.

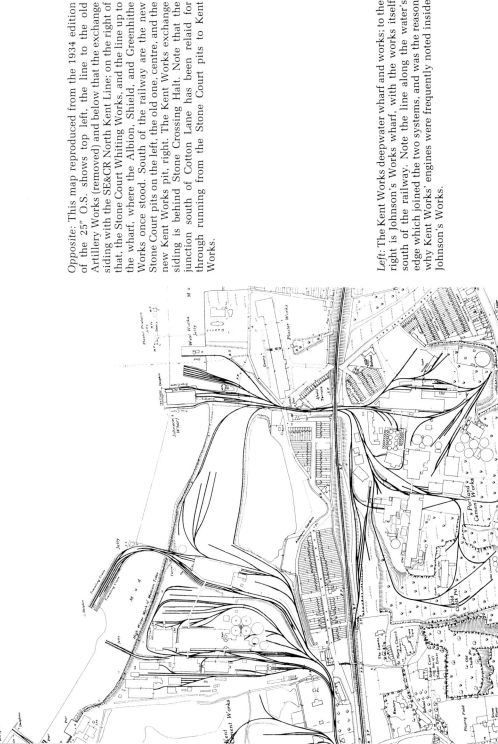

Left: The Kent Works deepwater wharf and works; to the right is Johnson's Works wharf, with the works itself south of the railway. Note the line along the water's edge which joined the two systems, and was the reason why Kent Works' engines were frequently noted inside Johnson's Works.

At the APCM Kent Works at Stone in April 1952; the engines are, *left to right, Clarence*, Peckett 1804, and *Arthur.*   *G. Alliez*

Clarence at Kent Works was a bit of a mystery; when this photo was taken in 1936 it carried only a rebuilding plate, but it is believed to have been built by Barclay in 1899.

R.D. Kidner

The Kent Works Hudswell Clarke 0–6–0ST *Stone* hauls 16 loaded wagons away from the face in the pit south of Elizabeth Street, Stone, in 1932. A similar, but empty, train (part is shown at the bottom) will be pushed to the face in its place; only the most powerful engines were used on this turn. *R.W. Kidner*

The Kent Works passenger carriage photographed in September 1933, in yellow livery with blue circles between doors; it was originally an LBSCR 1st/2nd composite (SR 5836). *R.W. Kidner*

The large pit south of Cotton Lane, Stone, in 1932 with the Atlas Stone Co. works established in the disused portion, and some extraction continuing at the far end.
R.W. Kidner

Kent Works *Hilton* photographed in September 1949. The engine, built by Peckett in 1896, came from the Hilton works at Halling.
G. Alliez

It should also be mentioned that two locomotives were borrowed in 1947 from neighbouring works:

Darenth	0–4–0ST	Peckett, 1741	1927	outs. cyls 14″ × 22″	3′ 2½″
		from BPCM Greenhithe			
	0–4–0ST	Brush, 277	1898	outs. cyls 12″ × 20″	3′ 0″
		from Stone Court Ballast Co. Ltd			

No. 7 was loaned to the Northfleet Works in 1945 for use in their chalk quarries.

As already stated, locomotives *Stone* and *Toronto* were scrapped in 1950. After that the steam locomotives were gradually displaced by diesel engines and have been disposed of as follows:

Arthur	Acquired in 1967 by the Kent & East Sussex Railway, Rolvenden.
Apex	Loaned to Kirton-in-Lindsey Works, 1949, 1950; scrapped 1960.
Hilton	Transferred in 1960 to BPCM, West Thurrock.
Elephant	Scrapped in 1960
Clarence	Scrapped in 1958
6	Scrapped in 1960
7	Sold in 1967 to Price (?), scrap dealers, Bexleyheath.
8	Sold in 1967 to Price (?), scrap dealers, Bexleyheath.
9	Scrapped in 1960

This works was replaced by the enlarged Northfleet Works in 1970; in 1973 some track and a few wagons remained, but not in use.

The tip-wagons used in the Kent Works quarries, which were fairly typical of those used elsewhere except in the most recent times, were as follows: inside bearing wheels, either cast spokes or built-up spokes, unsprung sub-frames carrying dumb buffers, above this a second frame on the non-tip side only. Three-plank wooden body with metal-braced corners, pivoted on the centre of three cross-members to the main frame, and with drop-sides on the tipping side only. The body was only marginally wider overall than the distance between the outside faces of the wheels, giving a total side clearance of about 5½ ft: this would not be possible of course with an outside-bearing wagon, and it was this combined with the simplicity of design which made them so popular. Some later metal wagons were virtually a copy of the above in sheet steel, but the wheels were only half the diameter of those on the wooden ones, fixed to a dropped frame, the round-ended dumb-buffers being mounted on solid angle-brackets to bring them up to the required height. It was noticeable that the bodies rusted through fairly rapidly. Neither type was braked; scotches would be used on the wooden wagons, but the metal ones must have relied entirely on the engine brakes.

The Kent Works was the only cement works included here which acquired a passenger carriage. This was an ex-LBSCR 1st/2nd composite six-wheeler, later SR No. 5836, and was probably purchased for the opening, certainly before 1930. It was painted in the official APCM livery for road vehicles, primrose yellow with blue circles between the doors and on the ends. It was kept in a siding where it would be handy for taking visitors from the road at Stone Crossing Halt up to the works, but was never noted in service.

I.C. JOHNSON & CO. LTD, GREENHITHE
579748

Isaac Charles Johnson was the 'Grand Old Man' of Victorian cement-making, living to the age of 100. After setting up the Crown Works at Frindsbury in 1851 in partnership with George Burge, he had formed the company I.C. Johnson & Co. Ltd in 1856 to operate a works in Newcastle. Returning to Kent, in 1872 he took over a quarry and tramway at Greenhithe which had been used to ballast sailing ships returning to the Far East without cargo. The tramway ran from the quarry, approximately where the works was later built, under the South Eastern Railway to a pier. The Johnsons' Works was opened in 1877; as I.C. Johnson did not purchase any locomotives, as far as is known, until 1891, he must have used those of his predecessor, but it is not known what they were, except that the gauge was presumably that used later, 3 ft 9½ in., the same as employed by the pioneer of clay railways in Dorset, Benjamin Fayle.

The original chalk quarries were just to the south of the works, with another to the west towards Stone church, but when these were exhausted it was necessary to tunnel under the Dartford–Gravesend road to open up new ones. These finally reached as far as the A2 London–Dover road, being worked on two levels; the top level was closed in 1952 and the lower level ultimately reached a depth of 200 ft.

The first step in modernising the works was taken in about 1903 when a rotary kiln was introduced. At about this time a line was laid to rise steeply to an exchange siding on the SE&C Railway to the west of the works. The Company joined BPCM in 1911. Then in about 1926 the works was closed for a time to enable it to be completely modernised and in the process of this reorganization standard gauge track was laid, as a temporary measure some of the line being dual gauge with three rails until the narrow gauge system was finally abandoned in about 1927. In 1928 one of the two lines running from the works to the pier was electrified on the overhead system, worked by motored bogie hopper wagons. These worked on 250V overhead supply, and carried a 25-ton load at 7 mph. They were built by English Electric (738–40) in 1928.

The modernised works included eight new concrete silos 96 ft high, and a new concrete packing shed on the jetty, which had an extension built out into the river so that larger ships could berth there. The three hopper wagons (two in use, one spare) acted as a link between silo and packing shed, running under the former to load up, and unloading at the jetty by means of compressed air and screw conveyors. They were remarkably silent-running.

Clay was at first brought by barge from pits on the Medway, but in modern times it was obtained from various local sites. For some time it was dredged from the river and the last duties of the locomotive Clinker were on the river bank in this connection. From 1920 until about 1964 the BPCM had a claypit at Bean (590718) with a 2 ft gauge railway there operated by Simplex and Planet locomotives. By 1930 clay was also being obtained from the APCM pits at Alkerden.

New Elephant at Johnson's Works, Greenhithe, was built by Bagnall in 1924 to the 3 ft 9½ in. gauge, and altered to standard gauge after the narrow system was abandoned in 1927. *F. Jones*

Johnson's Works *Darenth* was one of three Peckett 'Specials' delivered in 1927 with cut-down cabs and short chimneys for tunnel clearance. *F. Jones*

Johnson's Works used three electric bogie transporters, supplied by English Electric in 1927, to carry cement from the works to the wharf. The eastern line of the pair running under the North Kent Line across a level crossing to the wharf was equipped with overhead wire; the pick-up was by a bow on the transporter's cab roof. This photo shows a transporter passing the Lamb Inn running in reverse to the works in 1930.

R.W. Kidner

New Globe, a 1901 Peckett, came to Johnson's Works in 1929 from the Globe Whiting Works nearby in Greenhithe; photographed here in the long Castle Pit in 1937.

R.D. Kidner

These standard gauge tipping wagons photographed at the APCM Kent Works in March 1973, after the railway closed, were typical of the inside-bearing wagons used by so many pits. *R.W. Kidner*

The 1928 Peckett *Longfield* at Johnson's Works after modifications to chimney and cab to reduce height, in 1937. *R.D. Kidner*

On the old 3 ft 9½ in. gauge railway the following locomotives were employed:

Elephant	0–4–0ST			outs. cyls	
Cement	0–4–0T	Bagnall, 1344	1891	outs. cyls 9" × 14"	2' 9½"
Samson	0–4–0T	Bagnall, 1417	1892	outs. cyls 9" × 14"	2' 7"
Clinker	0–4–0ST	Falcon, 249	1897	outs. cyls	
Mammoth	0–4–0ST	Bagnall, 1582	1899	outs. cyls 10" × 15"	2' 9¼"
Leviathan	0–4–0ST	Bagnall, 1609	1900	outs. cyls 10" × 15"	2' 9¼"
	0–4–0WTG	Aveling, 4537	1900	compound cyls 8½" × 14⅛" × 14"	3' 6"
Goliath	0–4–0ST	Barclay, 1741	1921	outs. cyls 12" × 20"	
New Elephant	0–4–0ST	Bagnall, 2258	1924	outs. cyls 10" × 15"	2' 9¼"

No details of *Elephant* are available. The Aveling & Porter locomotive was transferred from the APCM works at Cliffe in 1920, and re-gauged from 3 ft 8½ in., but the remainder were all supplied new. In 1926 *Cement* was rebuilt at the Greenhithe Works with a Sentinel boiler and engine (No. 6220) with two vertical cylinders 6¼ in. × 9 in.

In 1927 when the narrow gauge system was replaced by 4 ft 8½ in. gauge track the following new locomotives were ordered to operate on it:

Stone	0–4–0ST	Peckett, 1740	1927	outs. cyls 14" × 22"	3' 2½"
Darenth	0–4–0ST	Peckett, 1741	1927	outs. cyls 14" × 22"	3' 2½"
Greenhithe	0–4–0ST	Peckett, 1742	1927	outs. cyls 14" × 22"	3' 2½"
Southfleet	0–4–0ST	Peckett, 1746	1928	outs. cyls 14" × 22"	3' 2½"
Longfield	0–4–0ST	Peckett, 1747	1928	outs. cyls 14" × 22"	3' 2½"

The first three were supplied with low cabs and boiler mountings, so as to clear the tunnels, being classified as 'Type W 6 Special' by the makers and looking very impressive with their very flat chimneys. The last two Pecketts were not cut down when delivered. They were however rebuilt at the works many years later to a similarly reduced height.

In addition to these new locomotives the narrow gauge locomotives *Goliath* and *New Elephant* were rebuilt to 4 ft 8½ in. gauge in 1927 by the makers and by the cement works respectively, and the following were transferred from other works:

New Globe	0–4–0ST	Peckett, 889	1901	outs. cyls 14" × 22"	2' 6½"
Globe No. 3	0–4–0ST	Peckett, 925	1901	outs. cyls 8" × 12"	2' 3"
Thames	0–4–0ST	Bagnall, 1588	1899	outs. cyls 12" × 18"	3' 0½"

The first two came from the Globe Whiting Co., Greenhithe, probably in 1929 and 1930 respectively, whilst *Thames* came from the abandoned Trechmann & Weekes Works at Halling in 1935, having been altered from 4 ft 2 in. gauge for the purpose.

Johnsons clay-pit at Bean was worked by two Simplex petrol engines and two Planet diesels; later by five Rustons diesels (175137, 182147, 194769, 195850/1); however they were often switched to other works and not always on site.

Of the narrow gauge engines, *Elephant* and *Samson* had disappeared by

This 1902 Peckett, *Globe No. 3*, was transferred to Johnson's Works from the Globe Whiting Works, also at Greenhithe.   *F. Jones*

The Bagnall engine *Leviathan* of 1900, narrow gauge (3 ft 9½ in.), laid up at Johnson's Works in 1932.   *G. Alliez*

Kerr Stuart's official photograph of *Globe* built in 1897 for the Globe Whiting Co. Ltd, and later *Globe No. 2*.   *B.D. Stoyel Collection*

Johnson's Works *Goliath*, rebuilt from narrow gauge to standard in 1927, seen here in 1937 running up the spur to the North Kent Line, which runs over the arches, one of the oldest features of the works and built by the South Eastern Railway before 1860.
R.D. Kidner

Johnson's Works *Darenth* shunting wagons which it has brought down from the SR
exchange siding, in 1930. The road level crossing by the Lamb Inn is behind the
wagons, and beyond is some waste land leading to the wharf.   *R.W. Kidner*

One of Johnson's narrow gauge engines, *Clinker*, built by Falcon in 1897, stands
derelict by the old clay-pond with a wagon of the same gauge, in 1932, five years after
the railway was converted to standard gauge.   *R.W. Kidner*

This narrow gauge Aveling & Porter geared engine came from the Cliffe Works; its gauge had to be widened by one inch! Seen here derelict in September 1932.

G. Alliez

Johnson's Works *Cement* was built by Bagnalls, but converted to a Sentinel vertical boiler geared engine in 1926; it is here seen derelict in 1936 in a corner of the works, where it lingered for ten years more.

R.W. Kidner

Goliath, a 1921 Barclay engine, was one of the 3ft 9½in. gauge engines at Johnson's Works which were regauged to standard in 1927; here seen in 1952.   *G. Alliez*

An impressive view of the large crescent-shaped Castle Pit supplying Johnson's Works, taken about half way down in 1930; this part has been worked out, and the one line is left in for trains to reach the pits to the south.   *R.W. Kidner*

1932, the Aveling was scrapped in 1934 and *Clinker, Mammoth* and *Leviathan* a year or two afterwards. *Cement* was not scrapped until after the war, although it had been derelict since 1927.

The standard gauge locomotives gradually became redundant during the post-war period until completely superseded by diesel locomotives. They have accordingly been hired or loaned out to other works, or otherwise disposed of, as follows:

Stone	Transferred to Frindsbury Works in 1962.
Darenth	Hired to Purfleet Wharf & Saw Mills Ltd in 1940–1945.
	Loaned to Kent Works, Stone, in 1947.
	Scrapped in 1963.
Greenhithe	Hired to Samuel Williams & Son Ltd, Dagenham Dock, in 1945.
	Transferred to Hessle Quarry, Yorkshire, in 1962.
Southfleet	Transferred to Frindsbury Works in 1960.
Longfield	Transferred to Holborough Works in 1960.
Goliath	Transferred to Grays Works in 1960.
New Elephant	Scrapped in 1960.
New Globe	Scrapped in 1960.
Globe No. 3	Scrapped in 1948.
Thames	Disappeared some time after the last war, no doubt scrapped: the cab and saddle tank were still visible in March 1952.

Lastly it should be mentioned that:

Tay	0–4–0ST	Barclay, 1828	1924	outs. cyls 12″ × 20″	3′ 2″

spent a short time at Johnson's Branch in 1942, having come from the APCM chalk pit at Highsted, before proceeding on loan to their Dunstable Works the same year. It returned to Greenhithe in 1946 and remained there until the following year when it was sent back to Highsted.

Along with most of the other remaining works in the area, Johnson's Branch was closed in 1970, production of cement being then concentrated at the new Northfleet Works and at Swanscombe.

JOHN TILDEN & CO., GREENHITHE
583751

A firm of this name operated the Lamb Wharf Chalk Works at Greenhithe in the 1860s, but very little is known regarding either the works or their railway. Presumably they excavated one of the long worked-out chalk quarries adjacent to Johnson's Works. Lamb Wharf is believed to have been on the site of the present enlarged Johnson's Wharf.

They had at least two locomotives of which the following meagre details can be given:

0–4–0WTG	Aveling & Porter, 48	1862	one cyl. probably 8½″ × 10″
0–4–0WTG	Aveling & Porter, 132	1864	one cyl. 9¼″ × 12″

Both these locomotives were supplied new and both were at work in November 1865. They were early chain-driven models and their eventual fate is not known.

GLOBE PORTLAND CEMENT & WHITING CO. LTD
588747

This pit at Swanscombe was originally opened up by J. & E. Hall & Co., before 1868, and was later in the hands of John Cubitt, Gostling & Co. who set up a whiting works to serve their Frindsbury Works. The company became the Globe Portland Cement & Whiting Co., and in 1899 the New Globe Cement Chalk & Whiting Co., at which time it probably moved to a new site to the east. In 1911 it joined BPCM. The Ingress Park siding from the SE&CR was laid in 1908. The original pit line ran from the Globe Wharf just east of Johnsons Wharf and under the SER and main road near where they crossed, to Mount Pleasant. Though the works closed in the 1920s, the wharf was later used for oil storage and some track was extant quite recently.

The early locomotive history of this firm remains rather obscure, but the following list summarises the details known to the writers:

Globe (?)	0–4–0WTG	Aveling & Porter			
Globe No. 2	0–4–0T	Kerr Stuart, 124	1897	outs. cyls 8½″ × 15″	2′ 3″
Globe No. 3	0–4–0ST	Peckett, 925	1901	outs. cyls 8″ × 12″	2′ 3″
Globe No. 4	0–4–0ST	Peckett, 967	1902	outs. cyls 10″ × 14″	2′ 6½″
New Globe	0–4–0ST	Peckett, 889	1901	outs. cyls 10″ × 14″	2′ 6½″

With the exception of the Aveling these locomotives were all supplied new to the Globe Company. The Aveling was reported to have been scrapped in about 1887, but this seems very doubtful. *Globe No. 2* is understood to have seen war service in France from 1916, returning to Greenhithe and being finally scrapped there. Another version is that two locomotives named *Globe No. 1* and *Globe No. 2* survived to be transferred to the APCM works at Grays, Essex, originally operated under the name of Gibbs & Co.; if this is true, it is possible that these two locomotives were respectively the Aveling and the Kerr Stuart in the above list.

The works was closed in the late 1920s, but three of the locomotives were still standing at the derelict works in 1929. They were subsequently transferred to other works of the Group, as follows:

Globe No. 3	to BPCM, Greenhithe
Globe No. 4	to APCM, Northfleet (No. 5)
New Globe	to BPCM, Greenhithe

Erith of White's Works, Swanscombe, built by S. Lewin in 1875, in 1921 after rebuilding in the Works. *Locomotive Publishing Co.*

J.B. WHITE & BROS, SWANSCOMBE
601753

The Swanscombe cement works was begun in 1825 by James Frost. He built a railway from his works north of London Road to a wharf described as 'upon a raised road across the intervening marsh' — probably the first line in the area. In 1833 a firm called Francis, White & Francis had a limeworks on the site of the new London & Southampton Railway terminus at Nine Elms in London; in 1837 the partners dissolved the firm and Francis & Son remained at Nine Elms, while White took over at Swanscombe Works, which had been run by the firm since 1833. In 1852 this firm became John Bazeley White & Bros.

Except that in 1883 it had become a limited company, the name remained the same until 1900 when the firm became one of the constituents of APCM (1900) Ltd. The processes carried out at Swanscombe were always charac-terised by a very progressive outlook and, despite their age, the works have been consistently modernised over the years. It is worthy of mention, that the first rotary kiln to be used in England on a commercial basis was put up at Swanscombe in 1901 having been manufactured in America by Hurry & Seaman.

The works lay to the north of the London Road and the tramway ran due north for 1000 yards to Bell Wharf. There was a whiting works to the west of the main works with a tramway to the pits near the cricket ground. The main pits were between the London Road and the South Eastern Railway. Some

A view of the Swanscombe Works in about 1905; two Taylor engines are coming in with a train of 15 wagons. *APCM Co. Ltd*

In White's Swanscombe pit in 1936; Fowler diesel No. 7 is on a loaded train, while *Kappa* waits with empty wagons. *R.D. Kidner*

For established faces, Whites used large steam navvies and railway-type wagons; here a train of chalk is passing through the loop near Knockall House on its way to the Swanscombe Works in April 1936. *R.W. Kidner*

Iron Horse was one of six side-tanks built by H.E. Taylor for J.B. White, this one in 1882; photographed in 1921. *Locomotive Publishing Co.*

The Falcon engine *Lion* was transferred from Stone Court to the Swanscombe Works in 1946, and is here seen in August 1947 working an upper gallery of chalk; the railway is not connected to the main line, which is running into a tunnel top centre; next year the engine was sold to Atlas Stone Co.   *R.W. Kidner*

Five of these engines were supplied by Hawthorns to Swanscombe Works in 1928 when the gauge was changed; this one, No. 6, did not however arrive until 1935.
John R. Bonser

time before 1898 the tramway burrowed under the South Eastern Railway in a tunnel at Craylands and pits were opened south of the railway later extending for a considerable distance. There was a transhipment siding on the South Eastern Railway at Craylands during the time of the narrow gauge. When the standard gauge line was built a single track ran down from the exchange sidings on a steep and curving route to the works. The standard gauge 'main line' ran through the tunnel under Craylands, then turned more westerly than the old line, and passed under a footbridge across old workings, through a tunnel under a lane, then another tunnel under Alkerden Lane, and into a very large pit running almost down to Watling Street, a distance of 1¼ miles from the Works.

Mr Frost laid a very early railway from the works across the marsh to a wharf on the Thames and this may account for the curious fact that, until replaced in 1929, the whole railway system in use around the works and quarries was laid to a gauge of 3 ft 5½ in. (sometimes given as 3 ft 8½ in.) and provided for the flanges to run *outside* the rails, thus complicating the arrangements at points. The reason is said to have been so that the space between the rails could be filled in solid to allow for 'horse traction'.

It is not known exactly when locomotive power was first introduced and there is some doubt about the identity of some of the stock, but it is believed that the following operated on this narrow gauge system.

Erith	0–4–0WT	Lewin	1875	outs. cyls 9½″ × 18″	2′ 6″
Gravesend	0–4–0WT	J.B. White		outs. cyls	
Revolution	0–4–0TV	De Winton	1881	two cyls 6″ × 10″	1′ 7″
Swanscombe	0–4–0T	H.E. Taylor	1879	outs. cyls	
Iron Horse	0–4–0T	H.E. Taylor	1882	outs. cyls 9½″ × 18″	2′ 6″
Dead Horse	0–4–0T	H.E. Taylor	1882	outs. cyls	
Millbank	0–4–0T	H.E. Taylor	1879	outs. cyls	
Liverpool	0–4–0T	H.E. Taylor	1879	outs. cyls	
Chester	0–4–0T	H.E. Taylor	1877	outs. cyls	
Plymouth	0–4–0TGV	Wilkinson	1884/5	two cyls 7¼″ × 13″	2′ 2″
Devonport	0–4–0TGV	Wilkinson	1884/5	two cyls 7¼″ × 13″	2′ 2″
Saltash	0–4–0TGV	Wilkinson	c.1884	two cyls 7¼″ × 13″	2′ 2″
Millbay	0–4–0TGV	Wilkinson	c.1884	two cyls 7¼″ × 13″	2′ 2″
Goliath	0–4–0WTG	Aveling & Porter, 3680	1896	one cyl. 8″ × 12″	3′ 0″
Jubilee	0–4–0WTG	Aveling & Porter, 3978	1897	comp. cyls 9″ × 14½″ × 14″	3′ 6″
Samson	0–4–0WTG	Aveling & Porter, 4176	1898	comp. cyls 9″ × 14½″ × 14″	3′ 6″
Galley Hill	0–4–0WTG	Aveling & Porter, 4469	1900	comp. cyls 9″ × 14¼″ × 14″	3′ 6″
Barnfield	0–4–0WTG	Aveling & Porter, 4501	1900	comp. cyls 9″ × 14¼″ × 14″	3′ 6″
Progress	0–4–0WTG	Aveling & Porter, 6040	1906	comp. cyls 9″ × 14¼″ × 14″	3′ 6″
Enterprise	0–4–0WTG	Aveling & Porter, 6419	1907	comp. cyls 9″ × 14¼″ × 14″	3′ 6″
Reliance	0–4–0WTG	Aveling & Porter, 6828	1909	comp. cyls 9″ × 14¼″ × 14″	3′ 6″
Swanscombe	0–4–0ST	Kilmarnock, 501	1920	outs. cyls 11″ × 16″	2′ 9″
Greenhithe	0–4–0ST	Kilmarnock, 508	1920	outs. cyls 11″ × 16″	2′ 9″
Northfleet	0–4–0ST	Kilmarnock, 507	1920	outs. cyls 11″ × 16″	2′ 9″
Hustler	0–4–0ST	Kilmarnock, 500	1920	outs. cyls 11″ × 16″	2′ 9″
Alkerden	0–4–0ST	Kilmarnock, 526	1925	outs. cyls 11″ × 16″	2′ 9″
Rede	0–4–0ST	Bagnall, 1413	1894	comp. cyls 9″ × 14″	2′ 7″
Spry	0–4–0ST	Hudswell Clarke		outs. cyls	

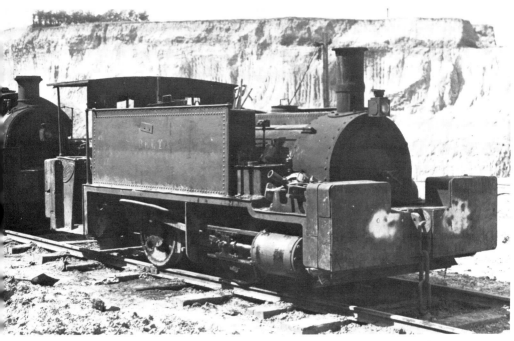

The Swanscombe Works engine *Delta* was one of a number originally supplied by the Falcon Engine Co., to Gibbs Works, Essex, with dropped cabs for tunnel work; here seen in May 1935, with *Kappa* behind. *G. Alliez*

Scaled side elevation drawing of *Delta*.

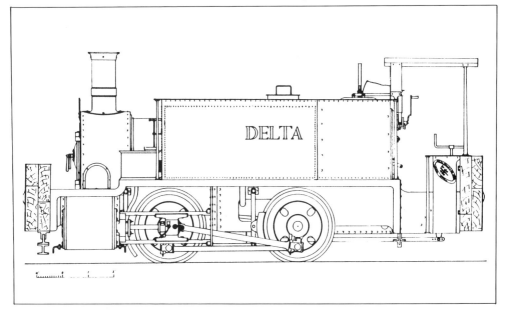

The only Manning Wardle engine at White's Swanscombe works was *Guernsey*, built in 1892, here seen under the steam shovel in the pit in 1937. *R.D. Kidner*

This Bagnall 0–4–0ST named *Rede* almost certainly worked on the Swanscombe system in narrow gauge days. It was built in 1894 for a 3 ft gauge waterworks railway, and it is not known when it arrived at Swanscombe. *B.D. Stoyel Collection*

It will be noted that one locomotive, *Gravesend*, was reputed to have been built at the Swanscombe Works and quite a number were rebuilt there at various times. *Erith* was a unique engine made by a Poole firm which produced very few engines. It had the eccentrics on the front axle and the valves were on top of the steeply-inclined cylinders, the spindles being actuated by Stephenson link motion. *Erith* was rebuilt at Swanscombe works in 1920 with the help of fitters from the Dorset Iron Foundry.

The majority of this very odd collection of locomotives were supplied new. The four Wilkinson engines were however purchased from the Plymouth, Devonport & District Tramways Co. and second-hand steam tram engines seem a curious choice for a cement works railway. There is some suggestion that *Revolution* came second-hand in about 1890 and possibly from the Bute Works Supply Co. Cardiff, who were advertising a similar locomotive for sale in 1893.

It is fairly certain that *Rede* and *Spry* came in 1921 and 1923 respectively, both second-hand. All the others are believed to have come new.

On a visit to the works in December 1929, 12 narrow gauge locomotives were seen on a length of track awaiting scrapping. The old 3-road engine shed was rebuilt as a two-road standard gauge shed.

On the modernisation of the railway system in 1929 all the remaining narrow gauge locomotives were scrapped that year or in 1930, and it is thought that very few of them had been scrapped at an earlier date, although *Plymouth* and *Devonport* are said to have been broken up in 1922, and *Swanscombe* by 1920. The second-hand engines would have had their gauge altered on arrival.

The narrow gauge wagons, wooden tippers, were shunted in 1929 into the passing loops half way down the tramway to the river, and remained there for many years. There were also a few left in an old pit south of Ingress Gardens.

When preparations were made in 1928 for replacing the narrow gauge system by one laid to the 4 ft 8½ in. gauge, an order was placed for a series of powerful new locomotives for the purpose. Pending their delivery three old locomotives were transferred from other works but they were usually employed two at a time in removing the overburden prior to quarrying, on track which had no physical connection with the remainder of the system. The complete standard gauge stock was as follows:

Wolf	0–4–0ST	Falcon, 120	1890	outs. cyls	
Guernsey	0–4–0ST	Manning Wardle, 1241	1892	outs. cyls 10″ × 16″	2′ 9″
Delta	0–4–0T	Falcon, 150	1887	outs. cyls 11″ × 18″	2′ 9″
No. 1	0–4–0ST	Hawthorn Leslie, 3715	1928	outs. cyls 15″ × 22″	3′ 5″
No. 2	0–4–0ST	Hawthorn Leslie, 3716	1928	outs. cyls 15″ × 22″	3′ 5″
No. 3	0–4–0ST	Hawthorn Leslie, 3717	1928	outs. cyls 15″ × 22″	3′ 5″
No. 4	0–4–0ST	Hawthorn Leslie, 3718	1928	outs. cyls 15″ × 22″	3′ 5″
No. 5	0–4–0ST	Hawthorn Leslie, 3719	1929	outs. cyls 15″ × 22″	3′ 5″
Kappa	0–4–0ST	Chapman & Furneaux, 1164	1898	outs. cyls 12″ × 19″	2′ 10″
No. 6	0–4–0ST	Hawthorn Leslie, 3860	1935	outs. cyls 15″ × 22″	3′ 5″
	0–4–0ST	Falcon, 205	1891	outs. cyls 11″ × 18″	3′ 0″
No. 7	0–4–0ST	R. Stephenson & Hawthorns, 7405	1948	outs. cyls 16″ × 24″	3′ 8″

A scene at the Swanscombe Works of J.B. White about 1905, showing Taylor and Aveling & Porter engines at work.   *S.A. Leleux*

This Chapman & Furheaux engine, *Kappa*, was built with low clearance for Gibbs of West Thurrock, and also worked at Frindsbury before coming to Swanscombe; note a new dome has been fitted. It is here seen in 1935 on an unconnected stretch of rail stripping overburden, or 'uncallow', from the top of a new chalk face.   *R.W. Kidner*

A vertical-boiler De Winton engine of 1881, *Revolution*, at Swanscombe in 1921.

Locomotive Publishing Co.

The vertical-boiler engine *Devonport*, built by Wilkinson in 1884, at Swanscombe in 1921.

Locomotive Publishing Co.

This design of Aveling & Porter four-wheels-driven geared engine was characterised by the long front overhang; note outside wheel flange; this is *Reliance* photographed at Swanscombe in 1921. *Locomotive Publishing Co.*

A similar engine, *Progress*, showing the gear-wheel side, on the same date.
Locomotive Publishing Co.

Wolf was transferred from Tolhurst's Works, Northfleet, whilst *Guernsey* and *Delta* came from Gibb's Works, Grays; *Kappa* was transferred in 1932 from the Crown & Quarry Works, Frindsbury; *Falcon* 205 came in 1946 from Stone Court Ballast Co. and was sold in 1948 to the Atlast Stone Co. Ltd at Stone. *Kappa* and *Delta* were built for restricted vertical clearance. Their Greek alphabet names were given by the first owner, Gibbs, West Thurrock, as was that of *Iota* at Stone Court.

In 1936 a Fowler diesel 0−4−0 (21455) was given the number 7, but in 1948 the number was re-alotted to a new steam engine, the diesel having been transferred to Alpha Cement, West Thurrock. Later Lister and Ruston & Hornsby diesel engines were also acquired.

Wolf was scrapped in 1945, *Kappa* probably in 1946, and *Guernsey* and *Delta* in 1947. No. 5 was loaned to Northfleet Works in 1955. In 1968 the frames of No. 5 were sent away for scrap and some of the parts were incorporated in No. 4, which then acquired the 'nickname' of No. 4½! In recent years, also, the saddle tanks of the six Hawthorn Leslie locomotives were interchanged to such an extent that it was said not one was carried by the locomotive to which it properly belonged. As the running numbers were painted on the tanks, the effect of these transfers was a virtual renumbering of Nos 1–6, but no attempt has been made in this account to follow these changes. It is gratifying to be able to add that no less than four of these locomotives have been preserved, and it is understood that these have all had their correct numbers restored. They are as follows:

No. 1	Ashford Steam Centre
No. 3	Quainton Road Railway Society, Bucks
No. 4	Sittingbourne & Kemsley Light Railway
No. 6	Middleton Railway Trust, Leeds.

The layout at Craylands Siding was altered, a long loop running down a steep grade from the BR siding through the 1906 tunnel in the NE corner of the pit to the Works.

To replace the steam locomotives, two diesels were brought in from Kent Works and two from Johnson's, after those works had closed. There was still some working of chalk faces for Snowcrete (white cement) and Snowcal (Whiting) up to early 1982.

APCM LTD ALKERDEN CLAY PITS, SWANSCOMBE
597737

Between Watling Street and Alkerden Manor Farm, not far from Swanscombe Wood, the APCM in 1909 opened up some extensive clay pits in connection with Bevans Works at Swanscombe. The clay was conveyed by rail from the pits to a collecting point nearby, where it was mixed with water and pumped by pipeline to the works. By 1930 clay was supplied from here to the Kent Works at Stone and the BPCM Works at Greenhithe also.

The railway in the pits was laid to 2 ft 8½ in. gauge, an unusual one but the same as the original railway at the Northfleet Works of Knight Bevan &

The Bagnall (1917) engine *Clinker* at Alkerden claypits in 1934; the track is sinking and the fireman is looking at a wagon which has just jumped the track.

L.T. Catchpole

The narrow gauge engines which worked the Alkerden claypits had mostly worked before at the Northfleet works of Knight, Bevan & Sturge. However, *Rocket* which was built in 1930 by Hawthorn Leslie, was delivered new to the claypit; photographed here in 1937.

R.D. Kidner

Sturge. A possible explanation is that when the Northfleet system was altered to standard gauge in about 1926, some of the track was relaid at Alkerden so that some of the equipment could also be transferred there. On the other hand the three oldest locomotives at Alkerden were said to have been there for some considerable time, so that the early history of the clay pits railways remains somewhat obscure. A small tramway layout adjacent to Southfleet Lane existed before 1900 and this may have been their origin. The tracks later wandered over a large area, serving mostly shallow pits. By 1933 they had reached the A2 Dover Road, and a long girder viaduct was built across the road, here in a wide cutting, to reach pits to the south of it. This was removed a few years later.

The locomotives were as follows:

Swift	0–4–0TV	Knight Bevan & Sturge(?)			
Rapid	0–4–0TV	Knight Bevan & Sturge(?)			
Alert	0–4–0TV	Knight Bevan & Sturge(?)			
Clinker	0–4–0ST	Bagnall, 2068	1917	outs. cyls 8″ × 12″	2′ 0½″
Meteor	0–4–0ST	Black Hawthorn, 1085	1893	outs. cyls 8½″ × 16″	2′ 6″
Planet	0–4–0ST	Hudswell Clarke, 631	1902	outs. cyls 8½″ × 16″	2′ 6″
Comet	0–4–0ST	Hawthorn Leslie, 3506	1921	outs. cyls 8½″ × 16″	2′ 6″
Rocket	0–4–0ST	Hawthorn Leslie, 3788	1930	outs. cyls 8½″ × 16″	2′ 6″

Very little is known about the three vertical boiler locomotives, all of which had been scrapped by 1931, but it is hard to believe that the names of the two first-mentioned ones were very appropriate! The Bagnall was obtained from C.J. Wills, Grimsby probably in 1921 when it was converted from 2 ft 6 in. gauge.

Meteor, Planet and *Comet* were transferred in 1928 from Bevan's Works, Northfleet. *Planet* was ordered from Chapman & Furneaux and carried their works plates (No. 1215, 1902) but this was the period when the firm was in difficulties, leading to its acquisition by Hawthorn, Leslie & Co. Ltd, and evidently the order was sub-contracted to Hudswell Clarke & Co. Ltd. *Rocket* was delivered new to the Alkerden pits. *Clinker* had gone by March 1943 and the remaining four, which were basically of the same design, were scrapped during 1943. The railway was superseded at about that time. Whites obtained clay from Cliffe from 1937.

ONWARD CEMENT CO. LTD NORTHFLEET
TOWER PORTLAND CEMENT CO. LTD
MACEROY & HOLT (BRITANNIA)
612749

These three works lying to the west of the Creek were supplied with chalk from quarries initially close to the works, but later south of London Road. Transport was handled by the Northfleet Coal & Ballast Co. Ltd who had a wharf there. A siding ran down from the up end of a loop in Northfleet SER station sidings, on a 1 in 40 gradient passing under London Road where was the locomotive shed and workshop. Trailing junctions from two large chalk pits (and the New Northfleet Paper Mills) came in from the left before the line passed across Stone Bridge Road and branched into several lines, namely (west to east) Onward Cement Works, the Tower Cement Works, the Deep Water Quay itself, and a cement works to the north of Grove Road. The Britannia Cement Works was located by the level crossing over Stone Bridge Road.

The gradient up to the SR exchange siding was so severe that it was customary to use two locomotives if the load exceeded 4 or 5 wagons. It seems probable that most production went away by river transport.

The Deep Water Wharf has not had a continuous history. It was apparently first opened in 1868 by the Northfleet Coal & Ballast Co. Ltd, whose business was then mainly concerned with coal delivery. At a later date they started to supply chalk, and no doubt the large pits north-west of the railway station were dug at this time. Not all the chalk was supplied to the cement works, however, and some was even exported to America. Later, when the supply of chalk was becoming exhausted, they opened in 1895 a second wharf and chalk quarries at West Thurrock on the Essex side of the Thames, which were operated under the name of the Thurrock Chalk & Whiting Co. The latter gradually superseded the Northfleet Wharf, the owners of which eventually went into liquidation. The Northfleet quarries were worked-out by 1920 and sold in 1921.

The business was revived by a company known as the Kent Deep Water Wharf Ltd and was later taken over by the Northfleet Deep Water Wharf Ltd. Probably the three cement works had been closed down well before this, and in modern times the wharf has been almost entirely dependent on the traffic of the adjoining New Northfleet Paper Mills Ltd. A new locomotive shed with workshops was opened in January 1953.

For so small a concern, or concerns, the locomotive stock was of exceptional interest and included two which were reputed to have come from main line railways. For simplicity the locomotives will all be listed together although there were two or three separate owning companies:

Peveril

Fly	0–4–0ST	Manning Wardle		outs. cyls	
Fox	0–4–0ST	Hy. Hughes	1871	outs. cyls 11″ × 18″	
Loughborough	0–4–0ST	Hy. Hughes		outs. cyls 9″ × 15″	
Northfleet	0–4–0ST	Hy. Hughes		outs. cyls 11″ × 18″	
Kilmarnock	0–4–0ST	A. Barclay, 282	1886	outs. cyls 11″ ×18″	3′ 3″
Swanscombe	0–4–0ST	A. Barclay, 699	1891	outs. cyls 11″ × 18″	3′ 5″
W.H. Davies	0–4–0ST	Brush, 282	1899	outs. cyls	
Torpedo	0–4–0ST	Peckett, 449	1886	outs. cyls 10″ × 14″	2′ 6″
Denis	0–6–0ST	Manning Wardle, 1561	1902	ins. cyls 12″ × 17″	3′ 0″
Dolphin	0–6–0ST	Manning Wardle, 725	1879	ins. cyls 12″ × 17″	3′ 0″
Bradley	0–4–0ST	Peckett, 1950	1938	outs. cyls 12″ × 20″	3′ 0½″
Victory	0–4–0ST	Dick & Stevenson		outs. cyls 14″ × ?	
Northfleet	0–4–0ST	Peckett, 2080	1946	outs. cyls 12″ × 20″	3′ 0½″

Of these *Fox, Loughborough, Northfleet* (Hughes), *Kilmarnock, Swanscombe, W.H. Davies, Bradley* and *Northfleet* (Peckett) are understood to

Outside the Northfleet Deepwater Wharf Co. engine shed in 1938; *Dolphin*, a Manning Wardle of 1879, is under repair; the tank and cab behind come from *Denis*, a 1902 Manning Wardle. Both engines later returned to service. *R.D. Kidner*

An 1886 Peckett engine, *Torpedo* on the Northfleet Deepwater Wharf system. *J.P. Mullet Collection*

have been supplied new by the makers. *Peveril* was a very old locomotive purchased second-hand from the Northfleet dealer, E.W. Goodenough, and reputed to have been built in the 1840s at the Edge Hill works of the Grand Junction Railway. *Fly* was stated locally to have come either directly or indirectly from the Isle of Wight and it is almost certain that it was in fact Manning Wardle's No. 111 which had been sent on test in 1864 to the Ryde Pier Tramway. *Torpedo* was bought from A.R. Adams & Son, of Newport, Mon., in 1920, and had been used in the construction of the GWR Wootton Bassett to Patchway line. *Denis* had been used by D. Shanks, a contractor, with whom it carried the name of *Coronation*, but is understood to have come from G. Shellabear & Son Ltd, Park Royal. *Dolphin* was bought in 1925 from the Southern Railway at Folkestone Harbour, No. A752, (possibly through George Cohen & Sons & Co. as agents) and had been rebuilt at the South Eastern & Chatham Railway's Ashford Works in 1911. The SE&CR purchased her in 1904, from W. Rigby, a contractor who did several jobs in Kent. Finally *Victory* came to Northfleet in 1942 on hire from the Ministry of Supply, their No. P234. It had previously been at the War Department depot at Kinnerley and left for an unknown destination, stated to be in Yorkshire, in 1943.

The following notes endeavour to show the fate of each locomotive so far as the Northfleet Wharf was concerned:

Peveril	Scrapped about 1900
Fly	Disappeared about 1919
Fox	Transferred from the old to the new Company about 1920 and scrapped in the early 1930s. At some time in its career this locomotive had acquired a new boiler by John Fraser & Co., of Millwall.
Loughborough	Transferred to West Thurrock about 1913
Northfleet	Transferred to West Thurrock about 1902–3
Kilmarnock	Transferred to West Thurrock about 1913
Swanscombe	Transferred to West Thurrock about 1913 (now preserved at Quainton Road)
W.H. Davies	Transferred to the new Company in about 1920 and scrapped in 1957
Torpedo	Scrapped in 1930
Denis	Scrapped about 1945
Dolphin	Scrapped about 1945
Bradley	Scrapped 1965
Northfleet	Scrapped 1967

KNIGHT, BEVAN & STURGE LTD, NORTHFLEET
619748

In 1853 a cement works was established by the firm of Knight, Bevan & Sturge between the centre of Northfleet and the river Thames, where lime had been made since Roman times. It continued to operate in this name until acquired as one of the constituent companies of APCM in 1900, although latterly Mr Thomas Bevan, DL, JP, had been sole proprietor. A certain notoriety attached to the works in 1880 when Mr Bevan, who was then MP for Gravesend, gave the employees of the firm a holiday with full pay on election day, an act which led to his being unseated by public petition.

Bradley, a Peckett of 1938, photographed at Northfleet Wharf in September 1949.
G. Alliez

The second No. 3 at Bevan's Northfleet Works, a 1931 Avonside, outside the works in 1934; the centre wheels have no flange. *R.W. Kidner*

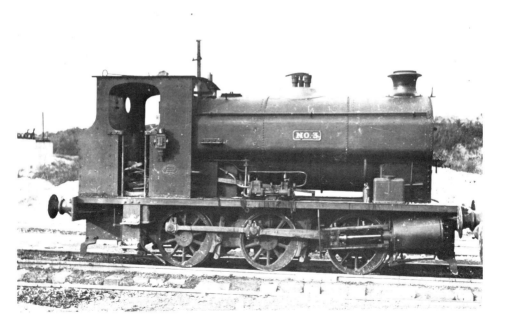

Maker's photograph of *Aerolite*, built by Black Hawthorn in 1893 for Bevan's Works at Northfleet.   *B.D. Stoyel Collection*

Maker's photograph of *Meteor*, built by Black Hawthorn in 1893 for Bevan's Works at Northfleet.   *B.D. Stoyel Collection*

Bevan's Northfleet Works converted to standard gauge in 1926; two new engines were delivered from Peckett of Bristol. Here Nos. 1 and 2 are being unloaded on 12th October, 1926 in Northfleet station yard, to be hauled to the works by the traction engine 'Black Prince'; the rail link to Perry Street Siding was not yet completed.

A.J. Martin

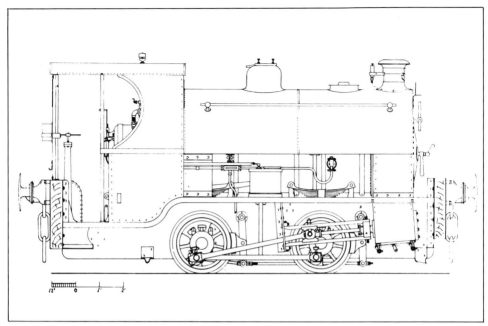

A scaled side elevation of Peckett No. 5 at Bevan's Works, Northfleet; *below*, a photograph of this engine at the Northfleet washery on 28th July, 1949.
(Both) G. Alliez

The British Rail entry to the new Northfleet Works complex in May 1977; the right-hand lines are for trains entering, and the left-hand for trains leaving.　　　D. Gould

Bevan's Peckett No. 2 hauling a full train from the wide pit at the south-eastern end of the Northfleet workings in 1934.　　　L.T. Catchpole

Quarries were opened to the south of the village and a 2 ft 8½ in. gauge railway was in operation between them and the works. This necessitated a tunnel under the high ground on which the High Street runs, and this is still in existence. The locomotives on this work were as follows:

		Neath Abbey I'wks	1874	cyls 8″ × 16″	
		Neath Abbey I'wks	1874	cyls 8″ × 16″	
Comet		Neath Abbey I'wks	1880	cyls 8″ × 16″	
	0–4–0WTG	Aveling & Porter, 952	1873	one cyl. 6″ × 10″	3′ 0″
Meteor	0–4–0ST	Black Hawthorn, 1085	1893	outs. cyls 8½″ × 16″	2′ 6″
Aereolite	0–4–0ST	Black Hawthorn, 1107	1894	outs. cyls 8½″ × 12″	2′ 6″
Satellite	0–4–0ST	Chapman & Furneaux, 1182	1894	outs. cyls 8½″ × 16″	2′ 6″
Planet	0–4–0ST	Hudswell Clarke, 631	1902	outs. cyls 8½″ × 16″	2′ 6″
Rocket	0–4–0ST	Hawthorn Leslie, 2649	1906	outs. cyls 8½″ × 16″	2′ 6″
Comet	0–4–0ST	Hawthorn Leslie, 3506	1921	outs. cyls 8½″ × 16″	2′ 6″

Aveling 952 was unique as it was of 4 hp only and the smallest built by these makers.

It is interesting also to note that all these locomotives were supplied new but that Planet was evidently built by sub-contract at the time when Chapman & Furneaux were in difficulties, as it carried their makers' plates (No. 1215 of 1902). Two of the locomotives were scrapped in about 1926 when the narrow gauge railway was superseded, whilst Meteor, Planet and Comet were transferred to the Alkerden clay pits in 1928 for further duties. There may also have been narrow gauge locomotives named Tolfa and Rota.

By 1925 the cement works, although partially rebuilt between 1903 and 1907, was out of date, but owing to the excellence of the river frontage a complete reconstruction was undertaken. This was finished in about 1926 and at the same time a 4 ft 8½ in. railway was laid down to connect with the chalk quarries through a tunnel some distance to the east of the original one. It also connected via various former trackbeds with the Perry Street siding of the former LCDR Gravesend West branch.

The rotary kilns installed in the reconstructed works were the largest in existence at that time, and new steam navvies were put to work in the quarries, each capable of excavating 150 tons of chalk in one hour. The system of operation was changed in that chalk was no longer brought to the works by the railway but was pumped by pipeline. A locomotive shed was built near the pumping plant but there was a second one adjacent to the works site where the repair shops were located.

The locomotives on the standard gauge system were as follows:

1	0–4–0ST	Peckett, 1701	1926	outs. cyls 14″ × 22″	3′ 2½″
2	0–4–0ST	Peckett, 1702	1926	outs. cyls 14″ × 22″	3′ 2½″
3	0–4–0ST	Peckett, 759	1899	outs. cyls 12″ × 18″	2′ 9″
4	0–4–0ST	Peckett, 829	1900	outs. cyls 12″ × 18″	2′ 9″
5	0–4–0ST	Peckett, 967	1902	outs. cyls 10″ × 14″	2′ 6½″
No. 3	0–6–0ST	Avonside, 2001	1931	outs. cyls 14″ × 22″	3′ 6″
Duvals	0–4–0ST	Bagnall, 1583	1899	outs. cyls 10″ × 15″	2′ 6″

These locomotives were somewhat unusual in having running numbers in the form of brass numerals in front of the chimney. Nos 1 and 2 were supplied new and although originally of identical design they were both altered at the Northfleet Works in different ways. No. 1 was fitted with an 'Aquastatic' water-softener and No. 2 was rebuilt with a rear bunker. This tended to upset its balance, so that it was again rebuilt in 1946. No. 3 came from Hilton's Works, Halling, No. 4 from Lee's Works at Halling in 1933 and No. 5 from the New Globe Works, Greenhithe (their No. 4). No. 3 (Avonside) was purchased through Messrs Cohen in 1934 from the Southampton Docks extension works for which Messrs Nuttall and Mowlem were the joint contractors. Being a six-coupled locomotive it was found generally unsuitable for the work at Northfleet and did not have a long life there; it was broken up in 1951. *Duvals* was purchased from the Grays Chalk Quarries Co. Ltd in 1951, but was scrapped in 1958. The first No. 3 was transferred to the Crown & Quarry Works at Frindsbury in 1934, No. 1 to the West Thurrock Works of BPCM in 1957 and No. 2 to Kent Works at Stone. The remaining locomotives were all scrapped, *Duvals* in 1958 and Nos 4 and 5 in 1966.

In addition, two locomotives were loaned from other works:

0–4–0ST	Peckett, 1985	1940	outs. cyls 14″ × 22″	3′ 2½″
0–4–0ST	Hawthorn Leslie, 3719	1929	outs. cyls 15″ ×22″	3′ 5″

These were borrowed in 1945 from Kent Works and in 1955 from Swanscombe Works respectively.

The railway was last used on 2nd September, 1964, being replaced by conveyer belting. The works closed in 1970.

Amid the welter of destruction in recent years, an odd survival was the few hundred yards of narrow gauge groove-rail tramway track in Grove Road, Northfleet. This was laid down some time before 1896 to serve a cooperage and whiting works, apparently on the west side of the Creek. The local council refused to allow this stretch of line to be opened, no doubt because, being laid as part of the cobbled road, it offended against some regulations covering street tramways. It is said that trains never ran upon it.

Peckett No. 1 at Bevan's Northfleet Works, photographed in 1947.   *G. Alliez*

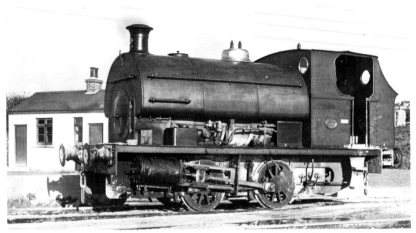

Peckett No. 2 at the Northfleet Works of Bevan's, one of two delivered new in 1926, photographed after the fitting of a rear bunker. *G. Alliez*

LONDON PORTLAND CEMENT CO. LTD, NORTHFLEET
623747

This works was opened in 1868 by J.C. Gostling and others, and sold in 1876 to the London Portland Cement Co. Ltd. This site was a little to the east of Bevan's Works at the Shore, Northfleet. There was a short tramway to pits north of the High Street. This was one of the constituents of the APCM on the formation of the latter in 1900, but it soon became redundant and was closed in 1908, by which time the tramway had been extended through a tunnel under Granby Road to pits and a brickworks at Calleybank. Latterly the system seems to have been integrated with that of the Crown Portland Cement Works lying just north-west. When the line serving Bevan's Works was opened in 1929 to the exchange sidings on the ex-LC&DR near Rosherville, it used part of this old line including the tunnel under Granby Road, as well as part of the route of another earlier tramway which ran from a point just north of the crossing of the LC&D over the SER, via a whiting works and a white lead works, to Red Lion Wharf. It is probable that the locomotive shed used by Bevan's Works was on the site of the London Works.

A short tramway from Calleybank to a pier on the river east of the London Works existed before 1875, but for what purpose is not known.

At least two standard gauge locomotives were employed in conveying chalk to the works:

Vulcan	Falcon	1884		
0–4–0ST	Manning Wardle, 651	1877	outs. cyls 9″ × 14″	2′ 9″

It is probable that *Vulcan* was supplied new but the Manning Wardle had originally seen service with the contractor William Moss in constructing the line between Peterborough and Seaton for the Midland Railway, at which time it carried the name *Stafford*. Its ultimate fate is unknown, but the boiler of *Vulcan* exploded in 1895 and it is likely that it was then scrapped.

RED LION CHALK & WHITING CO. LTD, NORTHFLEET
630745

A tramway was laid about 1860 from Red Lion Wharf, Northfleet, to some limekilns near London Road, east of Woodfield Lodge; by 1870 a tunnel had been built under London Road and the tramway was exploiting the chalk land between there and Old London Road. The early owner is uncertain; in 1896 Tolhurst & Sons Ltd registered the Red Lion Chalk & Whiting Co. Ltd to take over his line, engines, works, etc. The railway was pushed further south-east and linked to the London Chatham & Dover Railway at Perry Street Siding. In 1898 land was sold for the erection of the Imperial Cement Co. Ltd mills, which by agreement had to take its chalk from Tolhurst. This was built partly on land formerly owned by a white lead works. All these works were serviced by Tolhurst's standard gauge railway. The Red Lion Works was taken over by APCM in 1908 and closed in 1919; however part of the railway was used a few years later for a new entry to Bevans Works. The Imperial Works joined APCM in 1900 and closed in 1908, leading to litigation over the chalk agreement with Tolhurst which did not expire until 1948.
The following locomotives were used:

Bulldog	0–4–0ST	Manning Wardle, 13	1860	outs. cyls 8″ × 14″	
Wolf	0–4–0ST	Falcon, 120	1890	outs. cyls	
Lion	0–4–0ST	Falcon, 205	1891	outs. cyls 11″ × 18″	3′ 0″
Leopard	0–4–0ST	Falcon, 239	1896	outs. cyls 11″ × 18″	3′ 0″
Elephant	0–4–0ST	Brush, 287	1899	outs. cyls 10″ × 18″	3′ 0″

Bulldog was in Northfleet by 1871 in the ownership of J. Durden. All the locomotives were later transferred to other APCM works or associates as follows:

Bulldog	to Stone Court Chalk, Land & Pier Co.
Wolf	to Swanscombe Works
Lion	to Stone Court Chalk, Land & Pier Co.
Leopard	to Crown & Quarry Works, Frindsbury
Elephant	to Kent Works, Stone

TOLHURST & SONS LTD, GRAVESEND
641743

Tolhurst's also had an extensive railway serving its Gravesend works, of 3 ft 6 in. gauge, laid down in the 1860s or before; it ran from a wharf between Rosherville Pier and Clifton Marine almost as far as what was later West Street. There were three kilns at various points on the system. It was not extended very much, but when the LCDR arrived in 1886 it had to build four bridges near West Street station over branches of the tramway. The site of the works and quarries was later used by the Imperial Paper Mills. One locomotive was said to have been named *Diamond* and to have been sold to the Imperial Paper Mills in 1948.

The sail-powered trolley used on the Francis Works tramway after it closed; it was run down to the shore at Cliffe to dig worms and inspect the sea defences.   Mrs M. Foord

FRANCIS & CO. LTD, CLIFFE
723756

A cement works was built about 1861 on the marsh west of Cliffe by Charles Francis; it was set up north-east of Cliffe Creek and chalk was carried from the quarry inland by a canal, replaced about 1871 by a 3 ft 8½ in. gauge railway; later the 'old works' became a whiting works and a new Creek Works was built south-west of it, with a new wharf, later re-named Nine Elms Works when the company had left its London depot at Nine Elms. Apparently the whole of the cement production was despatched by river barge, there being no rail connection. The works were acquired by APCM in 1900 and closed in 1920.

The locomotives all appear to have been supplied new and were as follows:

	0–4–0TV	Chaplin, 985	1867		
	0–4–0WTG	Aveling & Porter, 915	1873	one cyl. 8″ × 10″	3′ 0″
	2–2–0WTG	Aveling & Porter, 1594	1880	one cyl. 8″ × 12″	5′ 0″
	0–4–0WTG	Aveling & Porter, 2229	1887	two cyls 5½″ × 10″	3′ 0″
	2–2–0WTG	Aveling & Porter, 2428	1880	one cyl. 8″ × 12″	5′ 0″
No. 3	0–4–0WTG	Aveling & Porter, 4360	1899	comp. cyl. 8⅞″ × 14⅛″ × 14″	4′ 0″
	0–4–0WTG	Aveling & Porter, 4537	1900	comp. cyls 8½″ × 14⅛″ × 14″	3′ 6″

The Chaplin locomotive was supplied through the agency of Wimshurst & Co., London, and was stated to be of 3 ft 7½ in. gauge.

The No. 2229 locomotive was not absolutely new when delivered, how-

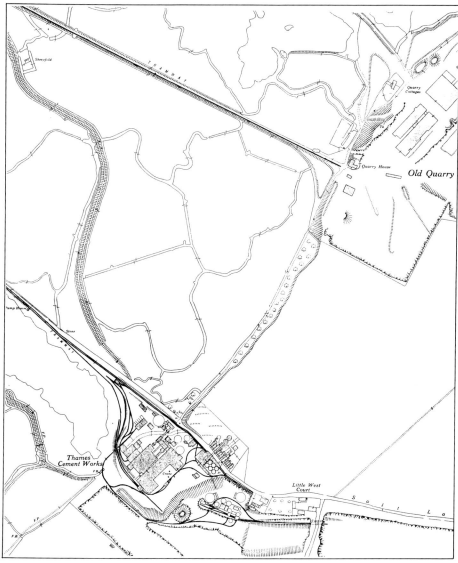

The eastern part of the Cliffe quarry complex from the 1934 25″ O.S. map. The straight track at the top is that which replaced the early canal from the inland quarry to the works at the mouth of the Creek, constructed in about 1861 by Francis & Co. Ltd. At the bottom is the works of Thames Portland Cement, later Alpha Cement; this tramway was 2 ft gauge whereas the Francis tramway was 3 ft 8½ in. Alpha later tunnelled under the road at Little West Court and opened a new pit north of the road.
Reproduced from the 1934, 25″ Ordnance Survey Map

ever, as it was supplied in 1890 and had an interesting background. It had been designed and built for work on the Brighton Tramways, but was found unsuitable and was returned to the makers, who rebuilt it in more conventional form. It retained its two high pressure cylinders, however, and in this respect was probably unique amongst Aveling & Porter's railway locomotives.

Nos. 4360 and 4537 were sent away in 1920 to Albert Batchelor Ltd at Halling, and the BPCM Works at Greenhithe respectively, where they saw further service. The others are believed to have been scrapped, although No. 2428 was still standing in the shed, out of use, until about 1938. There is an unconfirmed report that it was subsequently used as a practice target for anti-tank weapons, an unfortunate fate for such an interesting survival.

It is amusing to add that after the closure of the railway a local fisherman fitted sails to a wagon and used it as an unofficial means of transport.

THAMES PORTLAND CEMENT CO. LTD
ALPHA CEMENT, CLIFFE
720757

The Alpha Works was built in 1912 and acquired from Thames Portland Cement Co. Ltd by the Alpha Group in 1934; it was enlarged and a narrow gauge railway replaced an original ropeway. The Group was taken over jointly by APCM and Tunnel Cement in 1938, and wholly by the former in 1948. For a long time cement went away by river or by road to Cliffe station, but a siding to BR was built about 1960, and when the works closed in 1970 it remained in use for aggregate traffic. This joined the Grain branch near Lower Higham.

Motive power was entirely i.c., there being at one time as many as 15 locomotives at work, all Ruston & Hornsby diesels except for three Fowler diesels purchased from the Essex Waterworks, Abberton, (21293/4/5 of 1936, named *Abberton, Layer, Reldon*).

The Alpha Cement railway ran from the works one mile straight north-west to a jetty a few hundred yards south of those used by the old line. A branch ran round the south of the works to a large pit to the south of Salt Lane. At a later date this was worked out and the railway tunnelled under Salt Lane to reach a new pit which was very close to those worked by the former Cliffe Works.

A description of this works published in 1956 stated that it was still relying entirely on shipping for bringing in coal and taking away the cement.

Part Two
The Medway Estuary

GILLINGHAM PORTLAND CEMENT CO. LTD
791690

A cement works was erected at Danes Hill, Gillingham, in 1874, and was acquired in 1893 by John Bazley White & Bros Ltd, from the Gillingham Portland Cement Co. Ltd. Its tramway is said to have been of 3 ft 6 in. gauge. The company was taken over by APCM and closed in 1910. The works was reopened in 1920 under different management, but closed at the end of 1935 for two months, after which an Agreement with the Rugby Portland Cement Co. Ltd allowed it to be opened yet again; Rugby purchased it in 1938 and closed it soon afterwards. At this time it is reported that an engine called *Excelsior* transferred from Batchelors, Halling was still in the works.

QUEENBOROUGH CEMENT CO. LTD
907720

The Queenborough Cement Co. Ltd opened in 1882 and by 1896 had a short tramway down to a wharf and creek leading off the River Swale; a siding to the SECR was laid in 1904. The chalk pit also supplied a ceramics manufacturer, A. Johnson & Sons Ltd, established in 1908, which had a narrow gauge tramway. The Cement Co. did not join APCM in 1900 but had a five-year Agreement; in 1910 it joined BPCM. In 1908 the wharf was taken over by some industrialists from Cheshire, mainly for coal imports; they included Philip Speakman from Liverpool and Joel Settle from Alsager, and in 1930 they formed Settle Speakman & Co. Ltd. The company's involvement with cement was purely the transport of chalk from the East Kent Chalk Quarry Co. Ltd at Gillingham, and the movement of products to the wharf.

Later a large variety of locomotives worked for Settle Speakman; of interest here are two:

Name	Wheel arr.	Maker & Maker's No.	Date Built	Cylinders	Wheel Diameter
Success	0–4–0WTG	Aveling & Porter, 5082	1902	comp. cyls $8\frac{7}{8}'' \times 14\frac{1}{2}'' \times 14''$	4' 0"
No. 2	0–4–0WTG	Aveling & Porter, 7975	1913	comp. cyls $10'' \times 16\frac{1}{4}'' \times 14''$	4' 0"

Success had probably lost its name by the time it arrived from the East Kent Chalk Quarry Co. Ltd. No. 2 was new. The former was scrapped before 1930 and No. 2 in 1946.

BRITISH STANDARD CEMENT LTD, RAINHAM
823675

This short-lived works opened in 1912; it was operated by the British Standard Cement Co. Ltd, a subsidiary of E.J. & W. Goldsmith Ltd, making

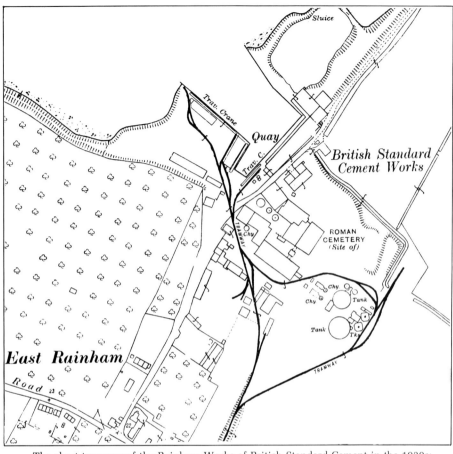

The short tramway of the Rainham Works of British Standard Cement in the 1930s;
the wharf was reached through Rainham Creek, and the line at the bottom passed
under the Gillingham Road into the pit.

Reproduced from the 1934, 25" Ordnance Survey Map

The 1913 Manning Wardle engine Venture had an unusual arched cab; it had been at
Wouldham Hall, but is here seen working on the Broom Bank line in 1937.

R.D. Kidner

'Capstan' brand cement. It was acquired in 1928 by the Red Triangle Group and then in 1931 by APCM, closing in 1937.

There was a 2 ft gauge tramway between the works and the chalk pit (possibly that at 820670), with the following locomotives:

	4–6–0T	Baldwin, 45142	1917	outs. cyls 9″ × 12″	1′ 11½″
Capstan	0–4–0ST	Bagnall, 2149	1925	outs. cyls 6″ × 9″	1′ 7″
Capstan II	0–4–0ST	Bagnall, 2262	1927	outs. cyls 6″ × 9″	1′ 7″

The Baldwin locomotive was acquired in 1918 from the War Dept Light Railways (their No. 560) and was rebuilt by W.G. Bagnall Ltd in 1918 before starting work at Rainham. The other two locomotives were supplied new and in 1933 were transferred to the BPCM Ltd's works at Beeding, Sussex. The Baldwin locomotive remained derelict at the works for some time afterwards and was then presumably scrapped.

EAST KENT CHALK QUARRY CO. LTD, GILLINGHAM
SHARPS GREEN CEMENT WORKS CO. LTD
811688

The address of East Kent was given as Gillingham, but this may have been just an office. It appears that the company owned a small chalk pit just north of the SECR at a place now known as Lower Twydall. A railway ran northwards under the main road at Sharps Green and on to the narrow peninsular forming the end of Bartlett Creek. Here Mr Alfred Castle had a wharf and barges to take chalk to his works at Queenborough; he also owned the quarry and the railway, but the cement works at Horrid Hill at the tip of the peninsular, known as Sharps Green Cement Works, was owned by C.L. Cary and B.P. Cary. It was opened in 1902, and taken over by APCM in 1910, being closed in February 1913.

Two Aveling & Porter locomotives were supplied new to East Kent:

Venture	0–4–0WTG	Aveling & Porter, 4612	1900	comp. cyls 8½″ × 14⅛″ × 14″	4′ 0″
Success	0–4–0WTG	Aveling & Porter, 5082	1902	comp. cyls 8⅞″ × 14½″ × 14″	4′ 0″

Venture had been sold by 1911 to the Sussex Portland Cement Co. Ltd, Beeding, near Shoreham (acquired by BPCM in 1911), and Success was later sold to Queenborough Wharf Co. Ltd.

SMEED DEAN & CO. LTD, EAST HALL, SITTINGBOURNE
926643

This works at Sittingbourne on the east bank of Milton Creek, near the village of Murston, was first set up by George Smeed in 1850 dealing mainly in bricks but later also lime and cement. Smeed Dean & Co. Ltd was formed in 1876. The undertaking joined the Red Triangle Group when this was formed and became part of APCM in 1931 when it took over the failed Red Triangle Group. The works closed in 1970.

A railway of 3 ft 7½ in. gauge ran from the East Hall clay pits, just west of Tonge Road, to some sheds and then on under Murston Road to the Smeed Dean complex. The following locomotives were employed:

0−4−2T	Kerr Stuart, 656	1900	outs. cyls 7″ × 12″	2′ 0″
0−4−0T	Kerr Stuart, 701	1900	outs. cyls 6″ × 10″	2′ 0″
0−4−2T	Kerr Stuart, 811	1903	outs. cyls 7½″ × 12″	?2′ 0″

All these locomotives were supplied new, but to different designs. The two earlier locomotives were scrapped in 1949 when the railway system was discontinued, but the 1903 one remained in storage in its shed until it was finally broken up in 1957.

BROOM BANK
927645

The Broom Bank railway, of 4 ft 3 in. gauge opened in 1933, ran from just north of the Smeed Dean cement works eastwards to East Hall, then north through Mere Court to clay pits near Little Murston, about 1¼ miles. Although close to the Tonge line at East Hall, there was no connection as the lines were of different gauge. The following locomotives were employed:

Wouldham	0−4−0ST	Barclay, 1679	1920	outs. cyls 10″ × 18″	2′ 6″
Venture	0−4−0ST	Manning Wardle, 1835	1913	outs. cyls 10½″ × 16″	2′ 8″

Both these locomotives were transferred from the BPCM Works at Wouldham Hall, in 1934 and 1935 respectively, and the rather unusual gauge was no doubt chosen for no better reason than the fact that these locomotives and other rolling stock happened to be available at the time. Venture was scrapped in 1949 but Wouldham lingered on to meet the same fate in 1962. Diesel locomotives were in use by 1956.

APCM LTD, HIGHSTED, SITTINGBOURNE
908620

Just north of the hamlet of Highsted, there was a group of pits whose railway was unconnected with any other, supplying chalk to the Smeed Dean works latterly through a large-bore pipeline, mixed with water. A pit to the east of Highsted road was opened first, about 1896, served by a narrow gauge railway. Later a larger pit the other side of the road was opened up, and the two were connected by tunnel. The railway was taken up in World War I and replaced in 1927 by a standard gauge line; this was also out of use in 1942−7. After re-opening, a third pit was opened up south of Tunstall Road, entered by a tunnel at the south-east end of the second pit, electrically worked.

The one locomotive was:

Tay	0−4−0ST	Barclay, 1828	1924	outs. cyls 13″ × 20″	3′ 2″

It was bought in 1927 from the Avonmouth contract of Sir W. Arrol & Co. In 1942 it was transferred to the BPCM Ltd's Works at Greenhithe and was almost immediately re-transferred to the APCM Ltd's Dunstable Works. It remained there until 1946 when it returned to Greenhithe and went back to Highsted in 1947. It remained in the chalk pit here until it was scrapped in 1962.

The equipment for the electrical working of the third pit came from the G. & T. Earle Hope Works in Derbyshire; there was a live centre rail taking 250V power from a motor generator. The three locomotives weighed 15 tons, with two 27 hp motors; two were built by Metropolitan-Vickers in 1927 and one in 1935 by Hawthorn Leslie. Trains of seven wagons took 56 tons of chalk from the pit to the old washeries, from which it was piped as slurry. Electric working started in November 1958 and ceased in 1970 when the works closed down.

There was an F.C. Barron & Co. cement works on the east side of Otterham Creek at 831675. There is no evidence of a railway at this works. Other cement works in this general area include Crown Quay Cement Works (F. Rosher & Co.) Sittingbourne; Dolphin Cement Works (C. Burley Ltd) on Milton Creek; Elmley Cement Works (later Maclean Levett), established about 1854 on Elmley Isle; there are no details of railways.

A general view of the Highsted pit on 15th June, 1957; note the newly-delivered electrical gear in the foreground; this is the west pit. G. Alliez

The Barclay engine *Wouldham* transferred in 1934 from Wouldham Works to the Broom Bank line, Sittingbourne; here seen in July 1948.   *G. Alliez*

Planet 3373 on the 4 ft 3 in. gauge Broom Bank railway on 15th April, 1957.
John R. Bonser

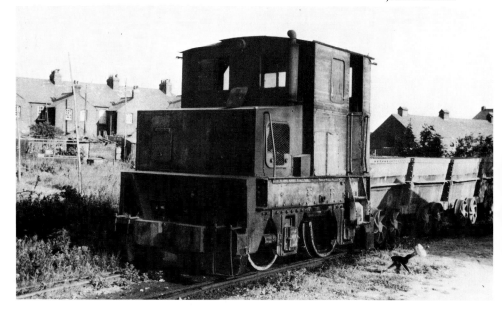

Maker's photograph of Kerr Stuart 701 at East Hall.   *Hunslet Engine Co.*

Kerr Stuart 811 at East Hall, Sittingbourne, on 6th June, 1948.   *G. Alliez*

Kerr Stuart 656 on the 3 ft 7½ in. gauge railway at the East Hall Works of Smeed Dean, Sittingbourne, in 1937. *R.D. Kidner*

The Highsted engine *Tay*; this photograph was taken in the west quarry in August 1935. *G. Alliez*

Highsted west pit on 15th June, 1957. The steam engine *Tay* was working the west pit, and one of the newly-delivered electric engines to work the south pit can be seen alongside.

John R. Bonser

The electrified track from the south pit at Highsted, with the washmills in the background, on the left of which an electric locomotive can be seen not yet assembled on its wheels. *Authors' Collection*

Two electric engines at the washmills at Highsted pit, seen with 8 cu.yd. tipping wagons, in 1958. *Authors' Collection*

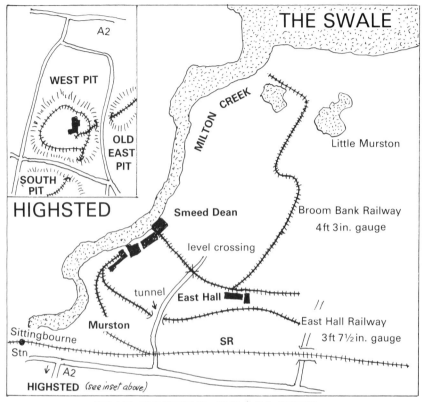

HIGHSTED (see inset above)

THE SMEED DEAN PITS

Two of the three electric engines at Highsted were built by Metropolitan Vickers in 1928; this is No. D2088, photographed on 15th June, 1957. *John R. Bonser*

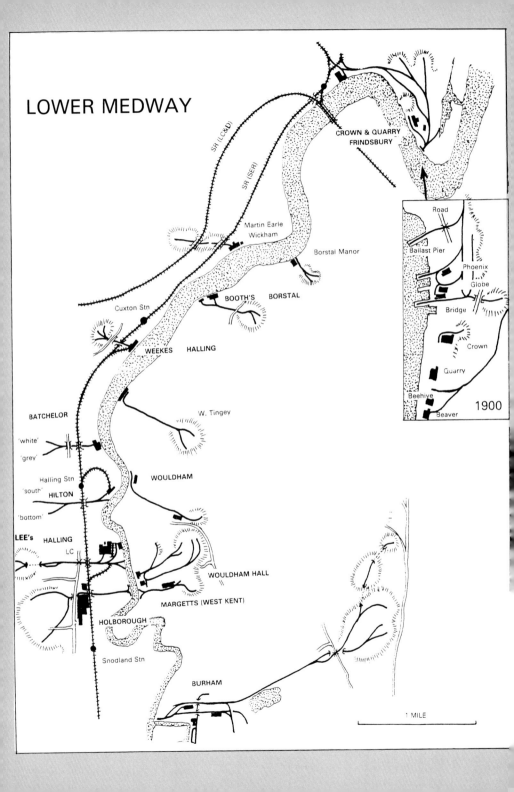

LOWER MEDWAY

SR (LC&D)

SR (SER)

CROWN & QUARRY
FRINDSBURY

Martin Earle
Wickham

Borstal Manor

BOOTH'S   BORSTAL

Cuxton Stn

WEEKES   HALLING

BATCHELOR

W. Tingey

'white'

'grey'

WOULDHAM

Halling Stn

'south'   HILTON

'bottom'

LEE's   HALLING
LC

WOULDHAM HALL

MARGETTS (WEST KENT)

HOLBOROUGH

Snodland Stn

BURHAM

1 MILE

1900 inset

Road

Ballast Pier

Phoenix
Globe

Bridge

Crown

Quarry

Beehive

Beaver

1900

Part Three
The Lower Medway

A further cluster of cement works, almost as complex as that between Dartford and Gravesend, was to be found on the lower Medway, roughly between the Rochester area and the limit of tidal waters near Snodland. It was originally entirely water-based, and tramways ran down from the chalk formations on both east and west banks to wharfs on the tidal mud. The result must have been a huge barge traffic before finally much of the traffic began to go away by rail. Because many of these lines had chosen unusual gauges, connecting to the South Eastern Railway's Strood–Maidstone line was not easy, and of course on the east bank there was no railway to connect with. All the tramways followed the same pattern: pits on the high ground, a descent to the works, and a wharf beyond. The length of the tramway depended on the configuration of the chalk formation.

Had one been sailing up the Medway at the turn of the century, one would first of all have passed on the west bank at the end of a creek the Whitewall Works of Formby Bros, using chalk from their Halling Works, but having no railway, and then on rounding the tongue of mud and turned north, in quick succession Beaver, Beehive, Quarry, Crown, Bridge, Globe and Phoenix; then turning south again and under the Rochester bridges, on the right bank the Wickham Works of Martin Earle & Co., with a short tramway under the SER and the converging LC&D line. Then a mile further on, Borstal on the east bank, followed immediately by Trechmann Weekes (west bank) and opposite it a tramway and wharf apparently used only to win chalk, with no works attached. Then came the Clinkham Works on the west, and the big Manor Works on the same bank, with the Wouldham wharf immediately opposite on the east bank; a quarter of a mile further, Lee's on the east and Wouldham Hall on the west were also opposite each other. A few chains south of Wouldham Hall came West Kent; the Snodland Works on the other bank, was of course not yet open. Then after navigating around the 'ox-bow' bend came the large Burham complex with its wharf on a further ox-bow quite close to the Eccles Roman Villa. This was the last of the group, we would be a mere 5 miles south of Rochester Bridge as the crow flies, but as the sailing barge went the journey from Burham to the Estuary, along a river winding continuously, and with winds fluked by surrounding hills, must have been an arduous trip.

At the height of activity here, the duties of the SE&CR pick-up goods must have been substantial, and some of the sidings required ground-frames to be installed. Though Earle's was worked from Wickham signal box, Trechmann Weekes had a ground-frame, also Batchelors. Hilton Manor was worked from Halling box, but there was a ground-frame for Lee's siding on the down side, almost opposite a later one on the up side, originally for a delivery siding called Medway Siding, but later still the north entrance to the Holborough Works sidings; the south entrance also had a ground-frame, though quite close to Snodland box.

This 1879 Manning Wardle engine, *Burham*, was transferred from Burham works in 1946 to the Crown & Quarry Works, Frindsbury, where it is seen on 8th April, 1950.
J.H. Meredith

This photograph from the Blue Circle archives shows an Aveling & Porter engine before 1900, tentatively identified as No. 1524 at Booth's Borstal Works.

APCM LTD, CROWN & QUARRY WORKS, FRINDSBURY
749691

Originally seven cement works were crowded on to less than half a mile of north shore of the Medway just downstream from Rochester Bridge. They were built on land belonging partly to the Rochester Bridge Wardens and partly to the Ecclesiastical Commissioners, and leased by William Tingey. He built the first, Crown Works, in 1851 and leased it to George Burge and I.C. Johnson; in 1875 he built Phoenix and set up the Phoenix Portland Cement Co. Ltd; in 1880 Globe was let to J.C. Gostling, Bridge in 1885 to the Bridge Cement Co. Ltd; Tingey built Beehive and Beaver works in 1890, and a year before that the Quarry Works had been set up by the Gillingham Portland Cement Co. Ltd.

Soon after 1893 Beehive and Beaver joined together as McLean, Levett & Co. Ltd. John Bazley White took over Globe and Bridge, and later Quarry, and in 1900 APCM took over the lot, splitting production into two groups, those south of Crown being called 'Crown', and those north becoming 'Quarry', the whole known as the 'Crown & Quarry Works'. Beaver closed in 1900, Bridge and Globe in 1901, and Quarry, Beehive and Phoenix in 1907. Four shipping berths were reduced to one, which was deepened, this was the former Crown pier.

Tingey had originally insisted that all the works except Crown use his chalk, some of which he obtained on site but much being barged in. However, the Ecclesiastical Commissioners appointed a quarrying agent, John Cole about 1863, succeeded in 1879 by William Ball, to work quarries on their land and to supply all the works except Crown, which had its own quarry. There were many disputes between Ball and Tingey, and times when all chalk had to be barged in. Ball continued to supply chalk to APCM until 1915.

During World War II the works was used for manufacturing fertiliser; however afterwards cement-making was stepped up and more pits opened. The works closed down in 1964.

At Phoenix there was a tramway to two piers from the quarries before 1869, at a time when all the chalk was barged away; there were two parallel lines, believed to be of 3 ft 6 in. gauge, horse-worked by John Cole. These were altered and extended to serve the Globe and Bridge works when opened. When the chalk near the river was exhausted, a tunnel under Quarry Terrace gave access to a quarry to the north, about 1885. A few years later some standard gauge track was laid south-east to the Beehive and Beaver works. This line was progressively extended, running on the north-west side of Commissioners Road, and in 1929 was joined up to the Southern Railway coal wharf sidings at Strood Canal Basin. The need for chalk led to quarries being opened east of Upnor Road and then by a tunnel to the west of it. The last one was dug about 1954. In its final form the railway was a broad 'U' behind the works, with a branch at the south-east and (where the locomotive shed was) to the new Crown & Quarry Works, which had replaced all the old ones.

The above account does not mention a railway operated by Tingey in his

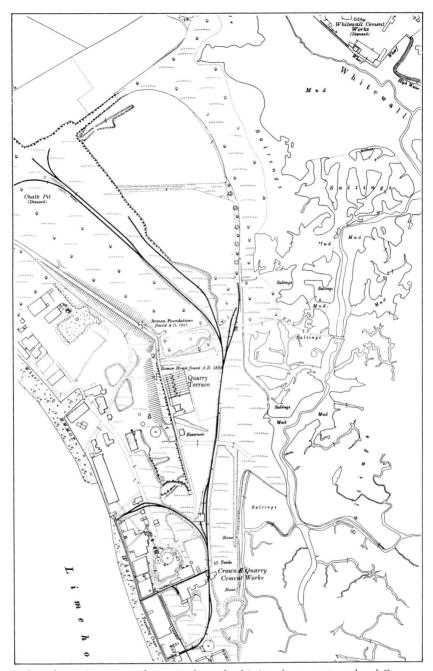

When this 25″ map was drawn in the early thirties, the cement works of Crown, Quarry, Beehive and Beaver had been amalgamated into the Crown & Quarry Cement Works, Frindsbury, Rochester. The Phoenix, Globe and Bridge Works had been further north, working small pits between the river and Quarry Terrace Road. Later, a branch from the northern loop shown here ran to a new works, the large rectangle marked here; also the pit line at top right was extended northwards, finally running under Upnor Road, out of this map to the north. Whitewall Works was never rail-connected. *Reproduced courtesy Ordnance Survey*

The Frindsbury engine *JGB*, built by Avonside in 1921, at Crown & Quarry in June 1955.   *G. Alliez*

George, an 1899 Peckett, which came from Northfleet in 1928 for a stay of over 30 years at Crown & Quarry, in its earlier condition, taken in August 1935.   *G. Alliez*

George, in its later form, with dumb buffers and altered chimney and dome-cover, seen at Frindsbury in June 1949.   *G. Alliez*

The Stephenson & Hawthorns engine *CFS*, built in 1952, and photographed at Frindsbury when new; note large diameter buffers.   *A.C. Baker*

own quarries; the gauge is not known, and its track difficult to observe on the maps around other lines, including Ball's. Two other adjacent cement works, Strood Canal Dock Works and Whitewall Creek Works, did not have tramways.

William Ball used locomotives in his chalk quarry; the following are known to have been supplied to W. Ball, I. Ball and I.H. Ball & Co.; but whether all were used at Frindsbury is not certain:

Name	Wheel arr.	Maker & Maker's No.	Date Built	Cylinders	Wheel Diameter
	0–4–0WTG	Aveling & Porter, 320	1868	one cyl. 8″ × 10″	3′ 0″
Burnt Oak	0–4–0WTG	Aveling & Porter, 447	1868	one cyl. 10″ × 12″	4′ 0″
Alderman	0–4–0WTG	Aveling & Porter, 3277	1893	comp. cyls 7″ × 11½″ × 12″	4′ 0″
Sabina	0–4–0WTG	Aveling & Porter, 4248	1898	comp. cyls 9″ × 14½″ × 14″	4′ 0″

Alderman was scrapped about 1915; the fate of the others is not known. The following locomotives are known to have been used at the Crown & Quarry Works:

Leopard	0–4–0ST	Falcon, 239	1896	outs. cyls	
Stuart No. 7	0–4–0ST	Barclay, 681	1890	outs. cyls 9″ × 18″	2′ 9″
Kappa	0–4–0ST	Chapman & Furneaux, 1164	1898	outs. cyls 12″ × 19″	2′ 10″
	2–2–0WTG	Aveling & Porter, 1524	1879	one cyl. 7″ × 10″	5′ 0″
Killarney	0–6–0ST	Hudswell Clarke, 611	1902	ins. cyls 12″ × 18″	3′ 1″
George	0–4–0ST	Peckett, 759	1899	outs. cyls 12″ × 18″	3′ 0″
Aylesford	0–6–0ST	Manning Wardle, 1395	1898	ins. cyls 12″ × 18″	3′ 0″
J.G.B.	0–4–0ST	Avonside, 1874	1921	outs. cyls 12″ × 18″	2′ 11″
Burham	0–6–0ST	Manning Wardle, 730	1879	ins. cyls 12″ × 17″	3′ 1″
C.F.S.	0–4–0ST	R.S.H., 7742	1952	outs. cyls 14″ × 22″	3′ 6″
Southfleet	0–4–0ST	Peckett, 1746	1928	outs. cyls 14″ × 22″	3′ 2½″
Longfield	0–4–0ST	Peckett, 1747	1928	outs. cyls 14″ × 22″	3′ 2″
Stone	0–4–0ST	Peckett, 1740	1927	outs. cyls 14″ × 22″	3′ 2½″

Stuart No. 7 was actually built to the order of Dick Kerr & Co. Ltd, and carried their plates with the date 1890 instead of those of A. Barclay Son & Co. *Killarney* was here on loan from Burham Works from 1934 until 1938. The only locomotive to be supplied new was C.F.S. The others were transferred from elsewhere as follows:

Leopard	c.1921	ex Tolhurst's Works, Northfleet
Stuart No. 7	c.1921	ex Anderson Brooks Works, Grays, Essex
Kappa		ex Burham Works
AP1524	c.1928	ex Booth Bros Works, Borstal
George	1934	ex Northfleet Works
Aylesford	1937	ex Burham Works
J.G.B.		ex Thomas W. Ward Ltd, Grays, Essex
Burham	1946	ex Burham Works
Southfleet	1960	ex Greenhithe Works (BPCM)
Longfield	1962	ex Holborough Works
Stone	1962	ex Greenhithe Works (BPCM)

The locomotives were disposed of as follows:

Leopard		Scrapped 1930
Stuart No. 7	c.1930	to Manor Works
Kappa	1932	to Swanscombe Works
AP1524		Fate unknown
George		Scrapped 1960
Aylesford		Return to Burham in 1938
J.G.B.		Scrapped 1964
Burham		Scrapped 1952
C.F.S.	1954	to Holborough Works and returned 1954
	1964	to Shipton Works, Oxfordshire
Southfleet	1964	to Thurrock Chalk & Whiting Co., Essex
Longfield		Returned to Holborough in 1962
Stone	c.1963	to Holborough Works

UPNOR CEMENT WORKS
751695

Just east of Frindsbury, a works was set up in 1858 by Hilton Anderson & Co. It was closed on acquisition by APCM about 1900 and became the Company's barge-yard. A photograph of it appeared in the Blue Circle 1900–1950 commemoration brochure showing five bottle-kilns in use; no details are known of any railway.

MARTIN, EARLE & CO. WICKHAM WORKS
725675

This works was squeezed into a narrow space between the hills and the river south of Rochester (Temple Marsh). Before 1900 it comprised a small pit between the LCDR and SER lines, and a 200 yds tramway running under the latter to a wharf. The gauge was 2 ft 4 in. and it was horse-worked. Later the tramway was tunnelled under both the former LCDR line and the nearby road, so that there were now pits between the two railways, between the LCDR and the road, and a larger one north of the road. There was a siding to the SER put in about 1899.

The first works was erected in 1881 by John Adams; in 1890 the Reliance Portland Cement Co. Ltd was the owner, but went into liquidation in 1895. Martin, Earle & Co. Ltd took over the following year and extended the works in 1899. They did not join APCM in 1900 but worked in agreement, joining BPCM in 1910.

In 1927 the gauge of the tramway was altered to 2 ft and self-propelled petrol-driven hopper wagons introduced (converted to diesel in 1956). The works closed in 1959 but was later re-opened using only road vehicles. Cement production ceased in 1968, and the works finally closed in 1970.

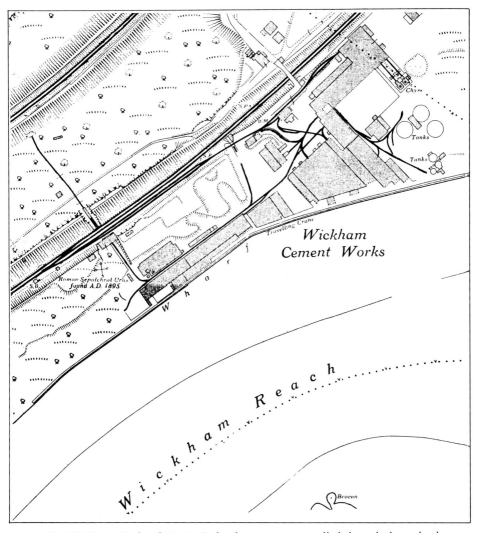

The Wickham Works of Martin Earle; the tramway tunnelled through the embankment of the ex-LC&DR line (*top left*) to a new pit to the north.
Reproduced from the 1934, 25" Ordnance Survey map

BOOTH & CO. LTD, BORSTAL COURT
723668

This small works was opened in 1852 by Edwin Hollick on the east bank of the Medway about a mile south of Rochester Castle. It was sold in 1866 to Samuel Booth, who converted six bottle-kilns into chamber kilns, and later took over a small works at Cuxton. Although closed shortly after joining APCM, 'Booth Brand' cement was still made for export long afterwards.

In its early years the Borstal Court Works was served by a short hand-worked tramway to the east of the works, by 1900 a longer railway had been built passing through a tunnel to reach the now-enlarged pits. Cable-haulage was considered, but may not have been used.

No physical remains of the railway have been visible for a good many years and not even its gauge is known for certain. There was however at least one locomotive:

2–2–0WTG Aveling & Porter, 1524   1879   one cyl. 7″ × 10″   5′ 0″

This had been supplied new to Booth & Co. and survived until after the closure of the works. It was finally transferred to the Crown & Quarry Works at Frindsbury for a few more years' service. The date 1928 has been mentioned for this transfer, but it seems more probable that it was earlier than this.

There has been some suggestion, from certain features of the locomotive's design, that the railway was a narrow gauge one, and as there was no connection with the main line railway this would have been feasible, but it is not thought to have been the case.

P.J. NEATE, BORSTAL MANOR
730671

A second cement works was started in 1894, a quarter of a mile north-east of Booth's Works, by J.L. Spoor, who failed, and the works was taken over by W.R. Craske in 1898, and later by P.J. Neate. It had a tramway some 300 yards long leading from the chalk pit to the works which were on the river edge. It may have worked chalk further inland, but its close proximity to the tramway to the prison makes this difficult to check. The pier and tramway incline immediately south-west of the Manor Works are believed to have served the prison only, although the existence on the 1898 6 in. O.S. map of formations marked 'old tramways' in the vicinity of the chalk pit east of Nashenden Farm must leave this open to doubt.

Midway between the Borstal and Wouldham pits there was a large pit east of the Wouldham Road at 715651. This had a tramway but no works, and may have been where Tingey got his chalk for barging to Frindsbury.

TRECHMANN WEEKES & CO., HALLING
706663

The first cement works at Whorne's Place, Halling, was set up in the 1850s by two men called Borman and Wild. T.M. Wild & Co. were running it ten years later, with Thomas Weekes as manager. The latter took over the business, joining with Otto Trechmann about 1892. A tramway about 600 yards long ran over the railway and under the main road to the quarry. Trechmann Weekes & Co. Ltd joined BPCM in 1910.

The tramway was of 4 ft 3½ in. gauge and the first two locomotives were the only rail engines built by Weekes & Co. of Maidstone, general engineers.

The rail connection to the SER is stated to have been put in in 1893, though the 1869 6 in. O.S. map shows what appears to be a connection. In 1910 one engine was working full-time on this siding, believed to be *Lioness* temporarily re-gauged. It was proposed to bring in an engine from Gillingham 'less powerful but suitable for station work', but in the end *Monica* was transferred from Formby's Works.

Details of the 4 ft 3½ in. gauge locomotives are as follows:

Leo	2-2-0WTG	Weekes	1877	one cyl.	
Lioness	2-2-0WTG	Weekes	1879	one cyl.	
Goliath	0-4-0ST	Bagnall, 1588	1899	outs. cyls 12″ × 18″	3′ 0½″

In about 1919, a standard gauge locomotive was transferred from the nearby Formby's Works:

Monica	0-6-0ST	Manning Wardle, 1538	1902	ins. cyls 12″ × 17″	3′ 1″

The SECR would not allow it to be run on their track, so it had to be brought by road. Short lengths of track were laid in the road in front of it and the short journey was accomplished in two days, with the engine belching soot and water from the chimney, according to a spectator of this unusual scene. This attempt at modernisation, however, did little to prolong the life of the works, which was closed in June 1921. *Leo* had already disappeared but the other locomotives remained on the site for many years. *Goliath* was transferred in about 1935 to the BPCM Works at Greenhithe, where it was converted to 4 ft 8½ in. gauge and renamed *Thames*. *Monica* and *Lioness* were eventually scrapped in about 1935 and 1937 respectively, having remained there derelict ever since 1921, one in the locomotive shed and the other in the tunnel under the road. The SR connection was removed in 1935.

RUGBY PORTLAND CEMENT CO. LTD, HALLING
704650

After World War II an entirely new cement works was constructed by the Rugby Portland Cement Co. Ltd, at Halling, very close to the site of Batchelor's Works.

Rather surprisingly, in 1966 the Rugby Co. transferred a steam locomotive to Halling from their Stanbridgeford chalk quarries in Bedfordshire, where it had been No. 7 in their fleet, a number still carried whilst in Kent. At Halling

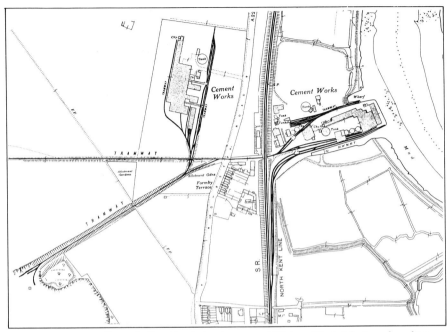

The works at Halling of Albert Batchelor, known as 'Clinkam Works', but much earlier as 'Formby's', in its final form in the 1930s.
Reproduced from the 1934, 25″ Ordnance Survey Map

Peckett 633 was supplied new to Hilton's Manor Works, Halling, in 1896. When the works closed, it was transferred to the Kent Works, where it is seen here in 1937, still carrying the *Hilton* name-plate.   *R.W. Kidner*

it operated on the standard gauge connection with the British Railways line between Strood and Maidstone.

Particulars are:

0−4−0TGV Sentinel, 9627   1957   2 cyls 6¾″ × 9″   2′ 6″

It did not have a very long life at Halling, being sold in 1969 to R.B. Tennent Ltd of Coatbridge, Lanarkshire.

There was a 2 ft gauge tramway within the works, worked by i.c. power.

ALBERT BATCHELOR LTD, HALLING
703650

Nearly opposite the present works of the Rugby Portland Cement Co. at Lower Halling, there is a row of cottages named 'Formby's Cottages', one of the few remaining links with a limeworks operated nearby by Charles Formby, at least as early as 1858. By 1878 the firm was known as Formby Bros and in 1881 it was registered as Formby's Cement Works Co. Ltd. There were two quarries at this period, the upper one containing white chalk which was burned for lime at the Halling Works, the lower one containing grey chalk which was shipped to the firm's cement works at Frindsbury. Each quarry was laid with railway tracks and normally one locomotive was in use at each. The only one traced is Aveling & Porter 0−4−0WTG 99 of 1863.

The company went into liquidation in 1909, and in 1911 a new company was registered, Albert Batchelor Ltd. The auction catalogue for the sale in 1909 mentions four locomotives, the details of which match what is known of Formby's engines, so it can be assumed that the new company took them over. The works, known as Clinkham Works, operated railways of three different gauges; it closed down in 1931 and was sold in 1936 to the Rugby Portland Cement Co. Ltd.

In 1936 the Rugby Company purchased the Rochester Cement Co. Ltd and in the Railway Clearing House Handbook the former Batchelor's Siding between Cuxton and Halling was so titled.

The following 4 ft 8½ in. gauge locomotives are known to have worked here:

	0−4−0WTG	Aveling & Porter, 99	1863	one cyl. chain driven	
Formby	2−2−0WTG	Aveling & Porter, 2078	1885	one cyl. 11″ × 12″	6′ 0″
Monica	0−6−0ST	Manning Wardle, 1538	1902	ins. cyls 12″ × 17″	3′ 1″
Albert	0−6−0ST	Manning Wardle, 902	1884	ins. cyls 12″ × 17″	3′ 1″

Aveling 99, 2078 and *Monica* were supplied new by the makers and in about 1919 *Monica* was transferred to the nearby quarries of Trechmann, Weekes & Co. Ltd travelling by road under its own steam. *Albert* is understood to have arrived at Halling before 1909. It had been used at one time by John Mowlem & Co. on a railway contract at Grays, but it is not known to the writers where it had been in the meantime. It did not remain long at Halling but was soon transferred to the Lewes Portland Cement & Lime Co. Ltd in Sussex.

The narrow gauge locomotives are much more uncertain, but the following are said to have worked here at one time or other:

Masham	0–6–2ST	T. Green, 366	1904	outs. cyls 9½″ × 14″	2′ 4″
Mena	0–4–0ST	Hudswell Clarke, 1019	1902	outs. cyls 6″ × 9″	1′ 8″
Excelsior					
Madoc	0–4–0ST	Avonside, 1467	1903	ins. cyls 8½″ × 12″	
No. 39	0–4–0WTG	Aveling & Porter, 4360	1899	comp. cyls	
				8⅞″ × 14″ × 14″	4′ 0″

Masham seems a most improbable type of locomotive to have worked here, but its presence is well authenticated. It had been supplied new to the Harrogate Corporation for use in connection with the construction of their Roundhill Reservoir and appears to have come to Halling from the War Department at Newbury at some time between 1922 and 1925. Its fate is unknown but it seems unlikely that it could have seen much service at such a restricted site. *Mena* was supplied new in 1912 to the Barry Sand & Gravel Co. through Robert Hudson Ltd of Leeds. This locomotive was built for the 2 ft gauge and was advertised for sale at Barry in October 1915, which is a reasonable date for its acquisition by Albert Batchelor Ltd. *Excelsior* is even more uncertain; it has been stated on doubtful authority that it remained at Halling until about 1935 and was then transferred to the Bulldog Cement Works at Gads Hill, near Gillingham. In June 1916 Albert Batchelor Ltd advertised a 2 ft gauge Kerr Stuart locomotive for sale and it seems likely that this was *Excelsior*, probably replaced by *Mena*.

Madoc was purchased in 1914 from Richard Thomas & Co. Ltd, Llanelly. The Aveling & Porter locomotive, which definitely ran on track of approximately 3 ft 9 in. gauge, was purchased in 1900 from the APCM Works at Cliffe. It was at work until the closure and was still on the site in April 1934. As far as is known it was the sole locomotive in use on the 3 ft 9 in. gauge railway here. *Masham* and *Madoc* were built to the 2 ft gauge and presumably were still of this gauge when in use at Halling, as was also probably *Mena*.

HILTON, ANDERSON & CO. LTD, HALLING
705639

The Manor works originally owned by Hilton, Anderson & Co. was in a relatively confined space between the South Eastern Railway and the Medway at Lower Halling, close to the Parish Church. A lime works opened in 1873 and the cement works in 1878. The quarries were in the North Downs just below Upper Halling and to the west of the railway line, necessitating a level crossing over the Strood–Snodland road. The operating company was Hilton, Anderson & Co., the name being changed in 1893 to Hilton, Anderson, Brooks & Co. Ltd, on combining with Brooks, Shoobridge & Co. Ltd. It was incorporated in the APCM Ltd combine in 1900. The works was closed in the late 1920s.

The first railway was laid to the unusual gauge of 4 ft 2½ in. and only one locomotive is known to have worked on it:

| Jessie | 0−4−0T | Appleby | 1880 | cyls 6″ × 24″ | |

Evidently this locomotive was not a success as it was advertised for sale in January 1881 after only 6 months' use.

On the 4 ft 8½ in. gauge railway which subsequently took the place of the original one, a number of locomotives were used. Details are in some cases somewhat obscure, but the following were amongst them:

Hilton No. 1					
Hilton No.2	0−4−0ST	Peckett, 829	1900	outs. cyls 12″ × 18″	2′ 9″
Hilton No.3	0−4−0ST	Peckett, 759	1899	outs. cyls 12″ × 18″	2′ 9″
Hilton No. 4	0−4−0ST	Peckett, 633	1896	outs. cyls 12″ × 18″	2′ 9″
Albion	0−4−0ST	Peckett, 915	1901	outs. cyls 10″ × 14″	2′ 6½″
Artillery	0−4−0ST	Falcon, 240	1896	outs. cyls	
Stuart No. 7	0−4−0ST	Barclay, 681	1890	outs. cyls 9″ × 18″	2′ 9″

Hilton Nos 2, 3, 4 were supplied new and the fact that their building dates are not in the same order as their running numbers suggests that they replaced earlier unknown engines. *Albion* and *Artillery* were transferred from the Artillery Cement Works Ltd, at Stone. *Stuart* came in about 1930 from the Frindsbury Works. This locomotive, although built by Barclay's, was apparently ordered by Dick, Kerr & Co. of Kilmarnock, and carried their plates. No. 3 was transferred to Northfleet Chalk Pits. No. 2 was later renumbered No. 3 and No. 4 was renumbered No. 1. Peckett 633 went eventually to the APCM Works at Stone, Peckett 829 and *Stuart* were transferred to the BPCM Works at Halling, in 1931, and *Albion* and *Artillery* to the BPCM Works at Penarth, Glamorgan.

WILLIAM LEE & SONS LTD, HALLING
708633

William Lee was in business as a lime burner at Halling in 1846, and in 1854 extended the business to include cement manufacture. In 1855 the works was trading as Lee, Son & Smith. In 1900 they were registered as William Lee, Son & Co. Ltd, and were in liquidation in 1912, the date at which the business was acquired by BPCM. The last Managing Director was Mr William Lee Roberts, the grandson of the original Mr Lee.

The works were situated about ½ mile south of Halling village and ¼ mile north of Holborough, lying between the Strood to Maidstone railway line and the river Medway, on which there was a wharf alongside the lime kilns. A 4 ft 3 in. gauge railway connected the works with a large chalk quarry to the west. The line passed over the South Eastern/Southern Railway, crossed the Strood to West Malling road (A228) by a level crossing, and after ascending for about half a mile to the mouth of the quarry it dropped very steeply to the bottom. There were two locomotive sheds, one just east of the railway bridge and the other at the entrance to the quarry.

The deserted wharf on the Medway at the long-closed Lee's Works, Halling, photographed in 1973. *R.W. Kidner*

The standard gauge engine *Stuart* (Barclay 1890) which had worked at Crown & Quarry, Frindsbury and Hilton's Manor Works, seen here working the standard gauge siding at Lee's Halling works in 1937. *R.D. Kidner*

Lee was one of the 4 ft 3 in. gauge engines at Halling working the line to the pits; it was photographed at the Lee's works on 4th June, 1938.   *A.W. Croughton, per F. Jones*

Sentinel locomotive 9627 of the Rugby Portland Cement Co. Ltd working at the former Batchelor's Halling works photographed on 20th September, 1969.   *G. Alliez*

Trains of empty wagons were hauled from the works to the entrance of the quarry, where there was a section of double track. In the meantime another locomotive would have brought up a train of loaded wagons out of the quarry to the adjacent track at the same point. Each locomotive then backed on to the train brought by the other one and made a cautious descent at the back of the train using considerable brake power. In addition a number of the wagons had their wheels 'scotched' for the descent.

The locomotives used on this 4 ft 3 in. gauge railway were as follows:

1	0–4–0TGV	Chaplin, 1940	1876	two cyls	
2	2–2–0WTG	Aveling & Porter, 1440	1878	one cyl. 10″ × 12″	5′ 6″
3	2–2–0WTG	Aveling & Porter, 1681	1881	one cyl. 11″ × 12″	5′ 6″
4	2–2–0WTG	Aveling & Porter, 1857	1883	one cyl. 11″ × 12″	6′ 0″
5	2–2–0WTG	Aveling & Porter, 3187	1893	one cyl. 11″ × 12″	6′ 0″
1	0–4–0WTG	Aveling & Porter, 4414	1899	comp. cyls 8⅞″ × 14½″ × 14½″	3′ 6″
Lee	0–4–0ST	Barclay, 1677	1920	outs. cyls 10″ × 18″	2′ 6″
Holborough	0–4–0ST	Barclay, 1716	1920	outs. cyls 10″ × 18″	2′ 6″

All these locomotives were delivered new, but the Chaplin locomotive was purchased through their London Agent, McKendrick, Ball & Co. This was a 15 hp locomotive and had an inverted engine, slightly inclined, working on to an independent crankshaft which was geared to one pair of wheels. It had a vertical cross-tube boiler. It is interesting to record that the second No. 1 was driven along the main road under its own steam when delivered by the makers from their works at Strood, a distance of some 3½ miles.

In addition to the above, the following locomotive was supplied new to Henry Lee & Sons, who were probably the predecessors of William Lee Son & Co. Ltd.

0–4–0WTG Aveling & Porter, 252   1867   one cyl. 10″ × 12″

The locomotives were scrapped as follows:

Chaplin	c.1900–1905
Aveling 1440	c.1930
Aveling 1681	1946
Avelings 1857, 3187	before 1930
Aveling 4414	January 1942 Sold for scrap to M. Lynch & Son, Rochester
Lee and Holborough	February 1941 Sold to Thomas W. Ward Ltd, Grays, Essex.

It is said that the two last-mentioned locomotives were purchased under the impression that they were of standard gauge and that the mistake was not discovered until their arrival at Grays, when they were scrapped.

After the narrow gauge railway had been in operation for a considerable period, a 4 ft 8½ in. gauge connection was put in between the works and the main line railway by a siding to the south of the works, with a third locomotive shed in between. Nos 3 and 5 and possibly No. 4 were converted

No. 3 at Lee's Works was an Aveling & Porter single-driver geared engine of 1881, photographed here on 8th August, 1935.　　　　　　　　　　　　　　　*G. Alliez*

A later four-wheels-driven Aveling & Porter of 1899, Lee's No. 1, photographed at the works on 4th June, 1938. Both these engines were of 4 ft 3 in. gauge.

A.W. Croughton, per F. Jones

Another Aveling & Porter 'single' photographed at Lee's Halling, probably No. 4.
B.D. Stoyel Collection

No. 1 at Lee's Halling was a vertical-boilered tram engine by Chaplin (1876); it was replaced by a second No. 1 in 1899. *B.D. Stoyel Collection*

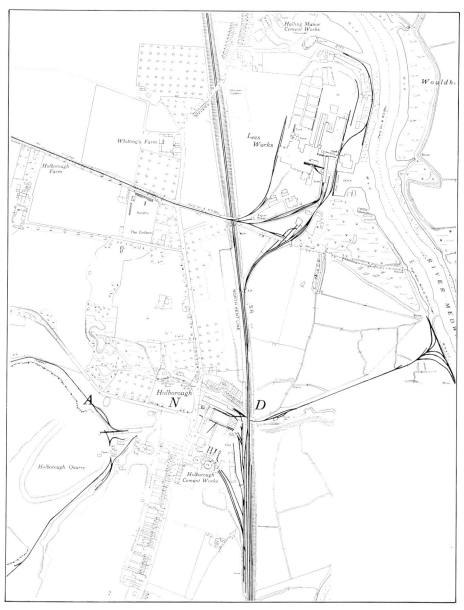

The Holborough Works in the early thirties; note the three separate systems of differing gauges; the pit lines, the line from the works to the river, and the standard gauge connections to the SR (a further connection was put in at the north end later). The Lee's Works line at Halling is shown to the north; the line passed over the railway but crossed the main road on the level. Right at the top, part of the former Hilton's Manor Works is marked. *Reproduced from the 1934, 25" Ordnance Survey Map*

to standard gauge, about 1900–6 and the buffing plate lifted to suit main line wagons. The following two further locomotives were later transferred from other APCM works:

| Stuart No. 7 | 0–4–0ST | Barclay, 681 | 1890 | outs. cyls 9″ × 18″ | 2′ 9″ |
| | 0–2–0ST | Peckett, 829 | 1900 | outs. cyls 12″ × 18″ | 2′ 9″ |

These are believed to have come respectively from Hilton's Works, Halling, in about 1930 and the Crown & Quarry Works, Frindsbury, c.1930. The Peckett was re-transferred in 1933 to the APCM Works at Northfleet. The Barclay was interesting in that it carried plates reading 'Dick Kerr & Co. Ltd, Kilmarnock, 1890', but it seems certain that they were Agents rather than builders in this instance.

The works were out of use by the time of the outbreak of war in 1939 and were soon taken over by the Royal Air Force as a depot. In May 1941 the RAF men lit a fire in Stuart No. 7, presumably because they wanted to take it for a drive, but there was no water in the boiler and considerable damage was done to the firebox. The locomotive was therefore transferred to Holborough Works in the hope that it could be repaired.

HOLBOROUGH CEMENT CO. LTD
706624

Many years after his company had gone into liquidation, Mr William Lee Roberts, the last Managing Director of Wm Lee, Son & Co. Ltd, founded a fresh cement works at Holborough, only ¼ mile to the south of his old works, which was constructed from 1923. The new company, of which he was Chairman, was known as the Holborough Cement Co. Ltd and was from 1929 associated with the 'Red Triangle' Group. It was acquired in 1931 by APCM Ltd and the works were still in production until 1983. They are situated in the rather restricted space between the Strood–Maidstone railway line and the Strood–West Malling road (A228). In the mid-fifties a new pit was opened at Paddlesworth, ¼ mile west, the clay being carried by telpher to the works.

The works are remarkable in having had three separate railway systems of three different gauges. The 4 ft 8½ in. gauge layout was within the actual works area, with connections with the main line both north and south, and both to the up line. The extensive chalk quarries are to the west of the main road and here was a 3 ft gauge system. These quarries gained a certain amount of public attention in 1952 because in expanding their extent a prehistoric round barrow, known as Holborough Knob, had to be destroyed. Finally the railway system in the quarries was relaid with 4 ft 8½ in. track, but it remained unconnected with the works system as the chalk is mixed with water and pumped by pipeline to the works. In this way the necessity has been avoided of having a level crossing over the road.

In addition there was a 1 ft 11½ in. gauge line running from the north-east corner of the works, under the main railway line and for about ¼ mile along a track leading to a quay on the river Medway, which was used in connection with the shipment of cement by barges. There was a separate loco-

The wharf line at Holborough Works was quite separate, of 1 ft 11½ in. gauge, and had its own locomotive stock; this is No. 2, a 1918 Bagnall, photographed by the tunnel under the SR in August, 1935. *G. Alliez*

The line in the pit at Holborough was 3 ft gauge; this Kerr Stuart engine, *Hawk*, was sent down from Warwickshire in 1931 but never went into service; seen here derelict in October 1932. *B.D. Stoyel Collection*

A 1937 scene in the Holborough chalk pit; the Canadian engine is bringing a full train
from the face, while two i.c. engines wait to propel their wagons up to the digger.

R.D. Kidner

This World War I 0–4–0ST built by the Montreal Engine Co. in 1917 is seen in June
1938 in Holborough pit.

A.W. Croughton

Felspar worked the standard gauge sidings at Holborough, having been acquired from George Cohen in 1937; it was a standard Manning Wardle design of 1914. Photographed in 1956. *B.D. Stoyel*

Tumulus was supplied new in 1954 from Stephenson & Hawthorns, and worked the standard gauge sidings at Holborough. *J.G. Brown*

motive shed a short distance to the east of the railway bridge. This system was entirely superseded a year or two before the last war, and all the railway systems went out of use about 1971. Rail transport was still used for finished cement, but coal deliveries were by a road vehicle from the Southfleet APCM coal depot, and chalk was carried from the quarry in the same way.

There were two connections to the SR line; both were trailing points on the up line; the one to the south, laid in when the works were built, ran down an incline to cope with the difference in levels. The north one, adapted from a war-time siding, left the SR slightly south of the connection to Lee's works and connected with a four-line 'gridiron' layout, probably for bulk cement tankers.

The quarry system was relaid in 1954 with 90 lb. flat-bottom rails; there was about ¾ mile of permanent track from the middle of the face around the washmills and lime plant, as well as some mobile track.

The standard gauge locomotives have been as follows:

	2−2−0WTG	Aveling & Porter, 9449	1926	one cyl. 11″ × 12″	6′ 0″
Hornpipe	0−4−0ST	Peckett, 1756	1928	outs. cyls 12″ × 18″	3′ 0½″
Felspar	0−4−0ST	Manning Wardle, 1846	1914	outs. cyls 12″ × 18″	3′ 0″
Stuart No. 7	0−4−0ST	Barclay, 681	1890	outs. cyls 9″ × 18″	2′ 9″
C.F.S.	0−4−0ST	R. Stephenson & Hawthorns, 7742	1952	outs. cyls 14″ × 22″	3′ 6″
Tumulus	0−4−0ST	R. Stephenson & Hawthorns, 7813	1954	outs. cyls 16″ × 24″	3′ 7″
Longfield	0−4−0ST	Peckett, 1747	1928	outs. cyls 14″ × 22″	3′ 2½″
Stone	0−4−0ST	Peckett, 1740	1927	outs. cyls 14″ × 22″	3′ 2½″

Of these, the Aveling, Hornpipe and Tumulus were supplied new, and, incidentally, the last-mentioned owes its name to Holborough Knob, to which reference has already been made. The Aveling locomotive was of a quite obsolete type by 1926, but Mr Roberts had grown up with locomotives of this design at Lee's Works and it is said that out of sentiment the first locomotive he ordered for his Holborough Works was of identical type. It was acquired in 1964 by the Bluebell Railway where its quaint appearance must occasion considerable public interest. Felspar was acquired in 1938−9 from George Cohen, Sons & Co. Ltd of Canning Town (their reference CP119); Longfield was transferred in 1960 from the BPCM works at Green-hithe, but spent a few months during 1962 at the APCM Frindsbury Works; C.F.S. came from Frindsbury Works in 1954 but returned within a short time. Stuart No. 7 was never used at Holborough, being moved from Lee's Works in 1941 with a damaged firebox and scrapped in about 1943. This locomotive carried Dick Kerr plates in place of those of the makers. C.F.S., Tumulus and Longfield were obtained for use on the quarry lines after conversion to standard gauge but the last-mentioned latterly took turns with Hornpipe as the works shunter. As there was no locomotive shed they were nearly always visible from a passing train. Stone was transferred from Frindsbury Works in about 1963 and scrapped in 1966. Hornpipe was moved for preservation to Quainton Road in 1972. For a few years before closure a diesel worked the standard gauge siding.

No. 3 on the wharf line at Holborough was this 1914 Kerr Stuart, which came from North Wales, and at one time had the odd name *Baby Senior*. *R.D. Kidner*

Hornpipe, one of the standard gauge engines at Holborough, was supplied new by Peckett in 1928; here seen in 1938, temporarily out of use and wedged between a chunk of concrete and a steam crane. *R.D. Kidner*

This Aveling & Porter 'single', now preserved, was supplied to Holborough new as late as 1926; its lack of a cab roof did not matter on this sunny day, 19th September, 1937.   *R.W. Kidner*

A much later photograph of *Hornpipe* at Holborough, in the siding beside the SR at the south end of the works in April 1958.   *John R. Bonser*

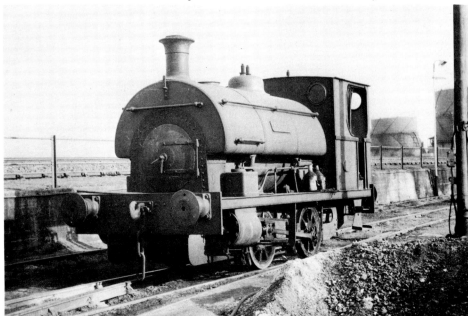

Only two steam locomotives were obtained for the 3 ft 0 in. gauge lines:

Hawk	0–4–2T	Kerr Stuart, 1213	1914	outs. cyls 7″ × 12″	
	0–4–0ST	Montreal, 54933	1917	outs. cyls 9″ × 13″	c.2′ 6½″

Both of these were second-hand; *Hawk* arrived in 1925 from the associated works of Greaves, Bull & Lakin Ltd at Harbury, Warwickshire. It had been rebuilt by the Hunslet Engine Co. in 1921. For some reason it was never used at Holborough and after standing in the open for several years it was scrapped in about 1938. The Montreal locomotive was of typical American design and was purchased in 1928 from the dealers Robert R. Paton Ltd of Cardiff. It was sent away for scrapping in 1953. For most of its existence the 3 ft 0 in. system was operated by internal combustion locomotives, (two O & K petrol, five Ruston diesel).
The following were the 1 ft 11½ in. gauge locomotives:

1	0–4–0ST	Bagnall, 2047	1918	outs. cyls 6″ × 9″	1′ 7″
2	0–4–0ST	Bagnall, 2073	1918	outs. cyls 6″ × 9″	1′ 7″
Baby Senior	0–4–2ST	Kerr Stuart, 1265	1914	outs. cyls 7″ × 12″	2′ 0″
No. 1	0–4–0ST	Kerr Stuart, 4290	1923	outs. cyls 6″ × 9″	1′ 8″

The two Bagnalls were acquired in 1926, but from where they came is un-certain. They had originally been supplied to the order of the Ministry of Munitions. They were scrapped in 1938. *Baby Senior* was transferred in 1928 from the Associated Ship Canal Portland Cement Manufacturers Ltd's quarry at Mochdre, Denbighshire, and scrapped in about 1940. No. 1 was purchased in 1939 from the South Essex Waterworks Co. at Abberton, where it had carried the name of *Midge*. It was never used at Holborough and was disposed of in 1940. A Ruston diesel locomotive and a Planet diesel were also used and later transferred to the Wickham Works. The engine shed and some track were still in place in 1978.

WOULDHAM CEMENT CO. LTD

A small works to the west of Wouldham village was started in 1855 by George Burge, but was in liquidation in 1859. In 1863 a new company was formed by Robinson & Gaskell Ltd, who purchased a second works at West Thurrock in Essex in 1874, which also became known as Wouldham Works. The original one however survived as Wouldham (Medway) Cement Works Ltd and joined APCM in 1900, closing in 1902.
It seems they operated a short 2 ft 8 in. gauge railway, for which a new locomotive was supplied:

0–4–0WTG	Black Hawthorn, 457	1879	one cyl. 4″ × 8″	1′ 8″

At a later period there was a 3 ft 6 in. gauge railway.
The only known locomotives were:

2–2–0WTG	Aveling & Porter, 2774	1891	one cyl. 8″ × 12″	5′ 0″
0–4–0ST	Fletcher & Jennings, 168	1879	cyls 8″ × 16″	
0–4–0ST	Bagnall, 1457	1895	cyls 6″ × 9″	1′ 6″

The A&P engine was of 6 hp and supplied new; the second was transferred about 1900 to the Wouldham Cement Co. Ltd, West Thurrock. The Bagnall locomotive is shown in Bagnall's records as having spare parts sent to the Wouldham Cement Works in April 1899, whereas in October 1898 spares had been sent for this locomotive to C. Baker. This previous owner is not identified, but he may have been the contractor of that name. Spares continued to be sent to APCM (1900) at the same address until February 1902, when the locomotive may soon have become out of use and scrapped or sold. There is a small doubt about this locomotive, as its original gauge was 4 ft whereas the narrow gauge at Wouldham was 3 ft 6 in. But it is doubtful what other works it could have been, described as 'Wouldham Cement Works'.

An old photograph, said to have been taken at Wouldham Hall in 1877, showing an Aveling & Porter engine, Victor, hauling a train of 26 loaded wagons.   T.B. Paisley

PETERS BROS, WOULDHAM HALL
712631

William Peters was making greystone lime at a works near Wouldham Hall, Burham, at an early date. In 1864 Edwin Peters went to Surrey to take over the Merstham Works from Hall & Co., and five years later Joseph Peters started building a new works at Wouldham Hall. This traded under the name of Peters Brothers Ltd. It was acquired by BPCM in 1912 and closed about 1925, though there were short periods of revival; because the products had to be barged across the river and carried to Snodland station costs were high. It was finally dismantled in 1938. The Peters family had a long association with the cement industry.

There was a 4 ft 3 in. gauge railway having two branches, the southern arm finally reaching the Scarborough Road at 720630; the southern one originally reached a pit through a short tunnel. At the riverside end there was a triangular junction, in the centre of which was the engine shed. The southern side of the triangle led to a short spur serving 'Margetts' Works. From here there was also a short incline down to a slurry pond. A separate 2 ft 6 in. hand-worked line brought coal from the wharf to a coal store.

The following locomotives are known to have been in use here:

Venture	2–2–0WTG	Aveling & Porter, 1199	1876	one cyl. 9″ × 10″	5′ 0″
Victor	2–2–0WTG	Aveling & Porter, 1342	1877	one cyl. 8″ × 10″	5′ 0″
Vivid	2–2–0WTG	Aveling & Porter, 1604	1880	one cyl. 9″ × 12″	5′ 0″
Venture	2–2–0WTG	Aveling & Porter, 2640	1890	one cyl. 9½″ × 12″	6′ 0″
Ninety Nine	0–4–0WTG	Aveling & Porter, 4402	1899	comp. cyls 8″ × 13″ × 14″	3′ 6″
Vulcan	2–2–0WTG	Aveling & Porter, 5441	1904	one cyl. 8″ × 12″	5′ 0″
Venture	0–4–0ST	Manning Wardle, 1835	1913	outs. cyls 10½″ × 16″	
Wouldham	0–4–0ST	Barclay, 1679	1920	outs. cyls 10″ × 18″	2′ 6″
Victor	2–2–0WTG	Aveling & Porter, 5603	1904	one cyl. 8″ × 12″	5′ 0″

It will be noted that by some whim, nearly all the names of the loco-motives begin with the letter V.

It appears that there were never more than five locomotives here at any one time and rather unusually all of them were supplied new, no doubt a necessary result of selecting such an unusual gauge.

Their disposal was as follows:

Venture	Aveling 1199) was returned to Aveling & Porter in 1899, in part exchange for *Ninety Nine*, rebuilt and re-sold to A.W. Itter of Calvert, Bucks.
Victor	Scrapped about 1933
Vivid	Sold in 1904 to Clarke Maylam & Co. (Lenham, Kent)
Venture (AP)	Sold in 1912 to Lewes Portland Cement Co. Ltd
Ninety Nine	Scrapped in 1938
Vulcan	Scrapped between 1932 and 1938
Venture (MW)	Transferred in 1935 to Broom Bank Clay Pit
Wouldham	Transferred in 1934 to Broom Bank Clay Pit.

THE WEST KENT (MILLBAY) WORKS, BURHAM
722624

This works was adjacent to Peters', just round the bend in the river, and was set up in the 1860s by J. Hallett, H. Haynes and W. Margetts, trading as the West Kent Gault Brick & Cement Co. It was officially known as Millbay Works, but right up to its closing it was always known locally as 'Margetts'. About 1890 the name was changed to West Kent Portland Cement Co. Ltd and the company joined BPCM in 1910. It closed at the end of 1925, but was re-opened two years later to make 'Continental' cement with high aluminium content; it closed again in 1931.

The kilns were on the river and a cable-operated incline ran up to a quarry. However a connection was later made to the Peters' railway near the locomotive shed and some material was supplied from Peters to Margetts.

BURHAM BRICK, LIME, & CEMENT CO. LTD
717608

Thomas Cubitt was working cement at Burham before 1859, when a partnership which included William Porter, later of the engine firm Aveling & Porter, purchased his works, trading as Webster & Co. In 1871 the undertaking was converted to a limited company under the title Burham Brick, Lime & Cement Co. Ltd. The works was taken over by APCM in 1900, and closed in 1930, but was re-opened in 1934 and finally closed in 1941. ·

The chalk pits were some way from the river and works and there was an extensive railway system; the 1900 pit near Scarborough required a tunnel, stated to have been 1600 ft long, under a lane and up to the slope of Bluebell Hill. The later pit was to the south of this and was worked at three levels, the top two by a gated level crossing over the Kits Coty to Burham Court road, with the lower level entry being by a tunnel underneath the level crossing. At the river end there were two wharves on a modified creek.

The locomotives included the following:

Medway	0–4–0WTG	Aveling & Porter, 4444	1899	comp. cyls 8⅞″ × 14⅛″ × 14″	4′ 0″
Rapid	(thought to have been 0–4–0ST by Manning Wardle)				
Burham	0–6–0ST	Manning Wardle, 65	1863	ins. cyls 11″ × 17″	3′ 1⅜″
Medway	0–6–0ST	Manning Wardle, 627	1876	ins. cyls 12″ × 17″	3′ 1⅜″
Burham	0–6–0ST	Manning Wardle, 730	1879	ins. cyls 12″ × 17″	3′ 1⅜″
Kent	0–6–0ST	Manning Wardle, 908	1883	ins. cyls 12″ × 18″	3′ 0″
Eccles	0–6–0ST	Manning Wardle, 1245	1894	ins. cyls 13″ × 18″	3′ 0″
Aylesford	0–6–0ST	Manning Wardle, 1395	1898	ins. cyls 12″ × 18″	3′ 0″
Killarney	0–6–0ST	Hudswell Clarke, 611	1902	ins. cyls 12″ × 18″	3′ 1″
Medway	0–4–0ST	Dick Kerr	1903	outs. cyls 10″ × 18″	2′ 8½″
Kappa	0–4–0ST	Chapman & Furneaux, 1164	1898	outs. cyls 12″ × 19″	2′ 10″

Of the above, Medway (A&P), Medway (MW), Burham (MW730), Kent and Aylesford were supplied new by the makers. Burham (MW65) had been built for W. Webster, of Plumstead, but it is not known whether it came from him direct, Eccles had been used previously by J.D. Nowell, the contractor, and was probably purchased by APCM in about 1902. Killarney had been owned by R. Finnegan, contractor, and had been in use with the Austin Motor Co. at Birmingham at about the time of World War I, but had arrived at Burham by 1919. Medway was apparently ordered from A. Barclay Sons & Co., but presumably they had too many orders on their books at that time as they sub-let the job to Dick Kerr & Co.

Nevertheless Barclay's affixed their own plates (No. 969 of 1903) before delivering the locomotive. It is said to have come to Burham from the other side of the Medway in about 1910 and to have been converted from 4 ft 3 in. gauge on arrival. It was used at a clay pit at a higher level. It had previously been owned by J.W. Ellis & Co. Ltd, Swalwell, Co. Durham, where it carried the name Reform. Kappa came from Gibb's Works at West Thurrock and also worked in the clay pit.

The fate of *Medway* (A & P), *Burham* (MW65) and *Medway* (MW627) is unknown. *Rapid* is said to have been scrapped in 1910, but it is doubtful whether it survived as late as this. *Burham* (MW730) was transferred to the Crown & Quarry Works at Frindsbury in 1946. *Kent* was scrapped by July 1943. *Eccles* was transferred to Dunstable Works by November 1934. *Aylesford* was transferred to Crown & Quarry Works in 1937, returning in 1938, and was scrapped in 1951. *Killarney* was also loaned to Frindsbury during the period 1934–1938, eventually being scrapped at Burham in 1951. *Medway* (Dick Kerr) had been sold to George Cohen Sons & Co. Ltd, shortly before March 1946, and it was subsequently re-sold to Roads Reconstruction Ltd, at Hapsford, near Mells, Somerset. *Kappa* was transferred to Crown & Quarry Works, probably in about 1930.

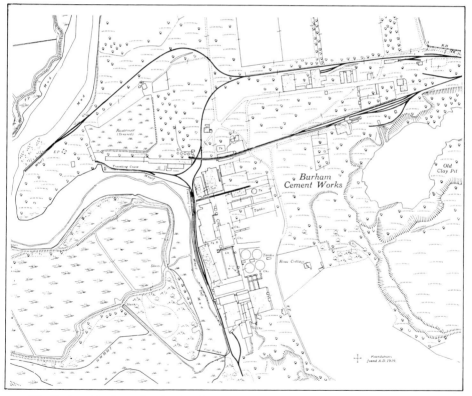

The Burham Works in the 'thirties; the topmost line continued east as far as Bluebell Hill, with pits being worked on three levels.

Reproduced from the 1934, 25″ Ordnance Survey Map.

The lower pit at Burham in September, 1937, with the locomotive *Killarney* hauling nine loaded wagons of the 'railway' type; these were braked, but had dumb buffers.
R.W. Kidner

Part Four

Today

The 1970s saw the final end of a process of rationalising the cement industry which had been going on for nearly a century. By 1880 it had become inefficient and almost suicidally competitive. Each works sought its own supplies of chalk and clay, and there was not enough mineral-bearing land to go round. Also, the adoption of the rotary kiln required a considerable capital investment; this could only be recouped by large-scale production, which in turn required larger reserves of raw materials. The formation of the 'combine' in 1900 allowed less favoured works to be shut, with the more favoured receiving rotary kilns. It was this trend, especially in the 1920s, which caused the replacement of narrow gauge by standard gauge lines, and the concentration of the industry into fewer but larger works requiring greater tonnages of raw materials.

By the 1930s there were just a few modern works: Kent, Johnsons, Swanscombe, and Bevans in the Thames heartland of the industry, and these served through the 1950s. At this time, APCM took a fundamental review of its UK manufacturing. One result was the building or rebuilding of a series of new, larger, regional works, mostly based on the more economic dry process of manufacture. These were at Dunbar, Weardale, Hope, Cauldon and Plymstock. This left the question of what to do with the life-expired Thames-side works. The solution was to build the world's largest cement works, based on the wet process; Northfleet, with a capacity of 3·6 million tonnes of cement per annum, opened in stages in 1970–1. To serve it, raw material supply was also rationalised; the Kent and Johnsons quarries were amalgamated into a single Western Quarry, and Swanscombe and Bevans into an Eastern Quarry. Bean clay was closed and replaced by Ockendon in Essex. None of these quarries now used rail transport to supply chalk for pipelining to Northfleet. Alone of the old works, Swanscombe was retained in operation, to manufacture special cements, and Swanscombe chalk continued to be supplied by rail from its particularly high-grade portion of the Eastern Quarry. This, the last chalk quarry railway, was not replaced by a pipeline until about 1979; Swanscombe still retains the nearest thing to a 'traditional' cement works railway system, although no longer serving either quarry or wharf. (The above notes were kindly supplied by Dr C.G. Down.)

The new Northfleet complex is served by a branch line of British Rail. This leaves the North Kent line near Northfleet station, then changes to right-hand running as the double line burrows under the main line. The right-hand line, for incoming empty and coal trains, then doubles and passes through a tunnel under London Road to reception sidings for cement empties and another for coal wagons. The line then passes through the works on a U-course, tunnels under London Road again, through a small pit and under Church Lane, to emerge as a double line some 30 yds west of the incoming line. This, the loaded train line, then singles to pass under the fly-under with the incoming line, and reverts to left-hand running to join the main line.

A 'merry-go-round' system of delivery and supply was inaugurated at Northfleet on 17th July, 1970, when BR class '33' No. 6595 pulled in with a train of gypsum from the Mountfield pits in Sussex. The plan included 21 coal trains per week to feed the kilns, nine trains of gypsum each of 17 wagons carrying 550 tons and up to 1,300,000 tons of cement leaving per year, in trains of 18 100-ton wagons. Whereas the gypsum was carried in aluminium-bodied hopper wagons, the cement wagons were on bogies, with two tanks of 'chevron' design for discharging under air pressure.

On 2nd March, 1968 British Rail withdrew their freight service to Perry Street siding, serving the cement works in Northfleet, and lifted some track, allegedly because they did not want the cement traffic. However in 1972 they agreed to lease part of the former Southfleet station and 1100 yds of track beyond to APCM for a concentration depot for coal to be trucked to the works. A small engine shed was built to house the locomotive doing this work, Royce/Sentinel 4w. diesel hydraulic of 1966 (No. 10260). At the time it opened, this depot served the following cement works: Johnsons, Bevans, Swanscombe, Cliffe, Holborough and the Wouldham Works in Essex. However latterly it served only the new Northfleet Works, Holborough and the remaining activity at Swanscombe. The depot closed in 1976 and was dismantled in 1981. In 1987 some of the track was removed to the KESR at Tenterden.

Appendix One
Personal Recollections

Of the handful of enthusiasts who roamed the cement railways in their heydey, few have left anything written down other than lists of engines. The many conversations with drivers and others were boiled down to the matter of locomotive history too. The following notes are therefore of great interest to anyone trying to recover the flavour of cement railway working. Oddly enough, in those days no one paid attention to strange young men with cameras; one could wander at will, though it was difficult to do so in the areas such as Northfleet where everything went on well below ground in tight tunnels and pits difficult to enter. Although the primary job on these railways was to convey chalk or clay from pit to works, there were always a great many engines around doing odd jobs: carrying workers or management on the footplate to somewhere, or pushing a single wagon with a mysterious load, or more often just standing waiting. This applied mainly of course to the large works; in small single-engine pits what went on was at least understandable to the onlooker. It is two such which are described in the first two notes, by Mr Colin J. Fleetney, who lived within sound of the Highsted pit, and whose father and grandfather had known Smeed Dean and their activities in Sittingbourne very well.

The Highsted Quarries

The first quarry, to the east of the Sittingbourne–Highsted Road was excavated by hand, gunpowder, and steam, to within 8 ft of that road, and to a depth of some 130 ft. A narrow gauge railway system hauled chalk from the faces to the crushing and slurry mills. The only road into the quarry consisted of a very steep and sheer-sided causeway, and to enable the railway to gain access to the workings to the north-east of the causeway it was pierced by a short concrete tunnel.

The quarry was worked intensively during the years 1896–1914. It was liable to waterlogging due to the fact that the floor level was considerably below that of Highsted Valley. To ensure continuous operation during the autumn and winter the railway track was, wherever possible, built on a low embankment, or timber trestling.

My father was convinced that during his childhood, that is from 1903 to 1913, there was one locomotive kept at Highsted. He visited the quarry frequently with his father, and recalled seeing what he believed to be a tall-domed 0–4–0 saddle tank, rather in the style of the slate quarry locomotives of Wales. The gauge was in the region of 3 ft. The trucks were of the then standard four curved-spoke wheel, heavy timber type. A steam excavator worked the hard south-west faces, standing for much of its time wheel deep in water. The excavator's gauge was, my father believed, 5 ft.

The slurry was pumped to the cement works at Murston, some three miles to the north, by way of an 8 in. cast iron pipe. A triple set of double-acting pumps, driven by a vertical, open, compound Ruston moved the slurry. Steam was supplied to all the stationary plant by a pair of Cornish boilers, with a square brick shaft, 80 ft tall.

The second quarry, destined to become the largest chalk quarry between Sittingbourne and the Medway, was started immediately to the west of the Sittingbourne–Highsted Road, adjacent to the first quarry, thus putting the road on a wide causeway. At first the overburden and the chalk was removed by way of a 2½ ton petrol 0–4–0 engine and a rake of steel tipping skips running on a 2 ft 6 in. gauge sectional line with pressed steel sleepers. Eventually the new quarry floor reached a level equal to that of the old quarry, and a tunnel was then driven through the causeway that supported the public road, connecting the quarries. The tunnel, still in existence, is brick lined and faced, and some 100 ft long. The tunnel, situated in the north-east corner of the new, or West Quarry, and now overgrown by trees, entered the East Quarry at its deepest point.

As the old narrow gauge railway system had been removed, together with most of the plant, during World War I, a standard gauge line was constructed to haul chalk from the new western faces to the slurry mill in the old pit. With its abandonment the floor of the old pit had been allowed to flood. The railway therefore left the tunnel and ran, at once, on an embankment between two large lakes, with an average depth of six feet. Silver birch trees lined the embankment, through which the train would move, almost invisible, during high summer, but for its exhaust steam. After World War II the lakes went dry, due to heavier water extraction by the Mid Kent Water Co. The silver birches then took the pit over until today it is virtually a forest. Once slurry mills and crushing plant were installed in the West Quarry, the plant in the East Quarry was allowed to become derelict, and the line through the tunnel was used infrequently.

The Barclay 0–4–0ST Tay was certainly the first locomotive I knew or heard, as I was born while she was working, and only half a mile from the quarry! The noise of this constantly hard-driven engine was part of my childhood, day and night. When Tay was not barking and slipping, the excavators were howling, or dull, solid thuds of blasting caused the village to tremble. There is not a house in Tunstall without cracked ceilings due to blasting in the quarry.

The trains usually ran from the mill, along the north side, and through a cutting, then round the great curved western face to wherever the excavator happened to be working. Tay then slowly eased her train along past the point where the jaws of the big electrically powered machine could dump into the trucks. Once loaded the train continued on, round the pit, under the southern face and back to the mill. The quarry was large enough for the vegetation to have taken a good hold to the rear of the workings. Thus the train ran through almost rural country, under the white cliff face. Seen from above, in high summer, the quarry was a picture of that pleasing combination that, sadly, only steam can enhance: industry and bucolic charm perfectly in harmony.

On nights of driving rain one could rest warmly in bed and listen to Tay slipping, slipping, slipping, as she fought to get her train moving from the face, on rails covered in creamy chalk mud. Night after night I have lain in the darkness willing her wheels to hold this time. I would count the beats; she was away! But no, with a clanging roar she would slip and stall. Gradually she would win, foot after foot, until one knew that she was doing perhaps a fast walking pace, and the exhaust would, to my boyish mind, sound triumphant.

We boys would, during the long summer holidays lie on the very brink of the south face and watch the smart blue and yellow locomotive with its train of lurching, swinging white trucks stagger beneath us, as clouds of sweet smelling coal smoke wafted up to us. Sometimes, very rarely indeed, the driver would whistle as he approached either end of his journey, and the glorious deep 'boom' of Tay's organ pipe whistle would rebound around the quarry. To our young ears a much superior note to the screech of a 'Southern' whistle down at Sittingbourne station!

In those days very rarely did the locomotive pass through the tunnel into the East Quarry. Indeed I cannot say why it should at all, because the mill was ruinous. I know that there were water supply valves situated in the old buildings, and no doubt it was easier to use the locomotive as transport when these valves had to be operated, than it was to walk the half mile or so. However, during school holidays we would sometimes dare enter the old quarry. It was very different from the scene in the West Quarry. It was vast, dripping, smelling of wet earth and leaf mould. The vertical cliffs, waterlogged railway earthworks and ruined engine house hinted at unspeakable horror. No birds seemed to sing, but there was always much rustling in the dense undergrowth. Part of the main engine house had collapsed, and the massive, rusting Ruston engine loomed like bones inside a vault.

Always our eyes were drawn to the distant black tunnel mouth at the end of the weed-grown track. Once while we wandered around, fearful of our own shadows, *Tay* lumbered without warning from the tunnel! We hid. The locomotive came with great care along the narrow embankment, between the lakes, and stopped close by us. The driver screwed the brake down and climbed down from the footplate. He entered the low door of the engine house basement, leaving *Tay* gleaming blue, yellow, and polished brass, quite out of place amid all the decay, to mutter and gurgle as is the habit of the steam locomotive. The driver banged around on some plant, closing valves and so on, while we cowered in the bushes. Finally he climbed back on to his patient locomotive which lurched and rolled, drain cocks gouting steam, through the silver birches to the tunnel. We were boys of that age, not this, and we fled!

I certainly remember the day that *Tay* arrived back at Highsted in 1947. During the war the entire APCM complex had just ticked over. A great deal of work, much of it maintenance, that was carried out had been undertaken by German prisoners-of-war. Indeed one group of these friendly and well-intentioned prisoners could frequently be seen driving the APCM's sole remaining Foden steam tipper between the works at Murston and the quarries. They kept that Foden in a splendid condition, and were usually good for a 'lift' if one admired the wagon sufficiently. *Tay* arrived back at Highsted on a low-loader, and certainly looked well. We watched as this seemingly huge locomotive nodded along, towering above our well-heeled suburban front gardens. We trotted alongside until the low-loader turned off the B2163 at Cromers Corner and gathered speed toward Highsted. The pit was coming to life again!

Again we were treated to powerful exhaust, to slipping and general hard usage of the locomotive, but night working was a thing of the past, as indeed was blasting. Gradually the quarry moved closer to the back gardens of the houses in Woodstock Road (the B2163) and the time came when it was impossible to work the western face any longer. It then became necessary to work the southern face up to the edge of the Tunstall–Highsted Road. This move resulted in the extinction of the 2 ft 6 in. gauge railway. Throughout the life of the quarry sections of this line had remained around the edge, indeed, about 200 ft of track hung from the north face like a huge necklace. The long abandoned and rusting locomotive, together with a dozen paper thin fragile skips stood on an isolated section of track, locked deep in a wild damson thicket above the south face; while along the brink at other points lengths of track could be found partly buried in the turf. However, the overburden above the south face was quickly and brutally removed by a fleet of huge modern machines within days, and the poor remains of the 2 ft 6 in. gauge train, together with its track were violated, and obliterated in minutes. A Roman burial ground found under the site of the damson thicket received somewhat better treatment, due to its national importance. Yet, after some three weeks this site too fell to the great yellow machines with their 9 ft tyres.

While work progressed on the newly opened south face a third quarry was started immediately to the south of the Tunstall–Highsted road. This quarry, roughly triangular in shape is cut into the rising ground from the valley floor toward the south-west. Access for private road and railway was gained via a modern concrete tunnel, about 80 ft long which passes under the Tunstall–Highsted road from the shallow south-west corner of the second, or West Quarry.

The steam locomotive *Tay* was by now nearing the end of her life. She was in an appalling condition, yet, as is the habit of steam plant, she continued to work in defiance of the accepted laws of engineering. The aged locomotive served the third quarry briefly, until the three electric locomotives appeared on the scene. When withdrawn, *Tay* was left for several years standing in an exposed position on a short spur of track out wide of the slurry mill, and could be plainly seen from the public road, a tiny black toy-like engine, forelorn in the vastness of the quarry. It was at this time that I attempted to purchase her, however, I could not meet the price offered by the men with the burning torches, so *Tay* went the way of so many other tired industrial locomotives.

The new South Quarry, with its green electric locomotives, did not last long. The workings were poor, with stratas of clay and sandstone, and in any case the houses which curtailed the working of the west face of the main quarry, were soon reached. Now the entire Highsted complex like the cement mills at Murston, which it supplied, is derelict.

Broom Bank Railway

I well recall the Barclay 0−4−0ST *Wouldham* busy, both in the mill and on the 'main line'. We boys would admire this blue and yellow engine frequently, but usually from far off. To stand at the 'Golden Ball' crossing, while perhaps one of those beetle-browed double-decked Leyland Titans beloved of the Maidstone & District Co. during the mid-1930s, a steam wagon, and other vehicles waited, was the highlight of a hot August afternoon. From the East Hall side of the road would come a ringing, and scrooping. Suddenly, moving at perhaps 15 or 20 mph *Wouldham* would come lurching and swinging down the slope, and across the main road. There was no question of slowing down, and I cannot recall a whistle sounding. There was, however, a flagman on the road. The wheels of *Wouldham* would usually be filthy, but her motion-work was a lovely oily red, and her crossheads stabbed at the road with a sense of tremendous power. She was followed across the road by her protesting jangling train, all red mud and clay. Once across the road the train swept, in grand style, round the sharp right hand curve, to vanish behind the houses, without decreasing speed.

Once in a while we would happen, as is the custom of boys, across the Broom Bank line in the woods, or close to the lakes. Here the well-maintained track, smelling of tar in the hot sun, seemed to be waiting for heavy traffic, traffic that, of course never came. We would play in the water and climb trees until dear old *Wouldham* came beating along, as she made her way between Murston and Little Murston.

During our time the Manning Wardle 0−4−0ST *Venture* stood, in an advanced state of decay, on a short spur of track just clear of the main line, on the works side of Murston Road. *Venture*, still blue and yellow, was almost lost under a huge growth of blackberry, and from her lace-like smokebox grew a substantial elder tree. It seemed an unkind fate, because the locomotive had been in a fair condition when abandoned. Her situation was strange in that while virtually backing on a public house, with a huge cement mill all around her, and a row of houses and shops close by, she stood in her grave surrounded by long grass, nettles, and large bushes. It was a sign of the times that she was complete, in that all her brass and copper work, whistle, injectors and so on, were in place.

Wouldham Hall Works

The following reminiscences are from the pen of the well-known railway historian, the late Arthur Ll. Lambert, who was brought up on the upper Medway and spent much time at the works usually known as Wouldham Hall, though in his day called 'Peters', and the next-door works of the West Kent Company, then and later known as 'Margetts', though marked on some maps as 'Millbay Works'. He describes the scene in the 'twenties. He returned in 1936 to find the works being destroyed, and out of curiosity came back again in 1975 after reading the first edition of this book, finding it difficult to associate the then-desolate pits with his boyhood memories:

'My paternal grandfather was associated with Peters Works from c.1890 until closure. Thereafter, he finished his time with Martin Earles, retiring in 1931. For many years he was an 'engineer' at Peters, but around the time of World War I there was a family quarrel which became a feud, the details of which were never talked about and, as a result, his brother faded out and my grandfather was demoted from the cement production side to become Foreman Cooper in an entirely isolated part of the works, towards the Wouldham village end (all the cement was then packed in wooden casks). My grandfather lived at first at Snodland but early in the present century moved to a company house built in late Victorian days on the overburden dump from the pit which served Margetts Works.

When I knew them the two works operated as one unit of BPCM and were both supplied from one chalk pit. They were in fact contiguous, being joined by a row of lime kilns. At the Margetts end were two disused chimneys of a different architecture from all the rest, one being a square structure, and presumably they were originals. At the Peters end of the gap was a grab crane over the river for dealing with the clay, an essential ingredient of the cement-making process. Originally here, this was taken direct from the river, as it was elsewhere on the Medway and is the reason why all the works were situated on the riverside, and presumably how the creek at Burham came to be enlarged so much. Later, the clay was imported by barge from elsewhere, but there was plenty of it about (the river was often referred to locally as the 'Mudway'), and hence the need for the grab crane. I think there was another grab crane inside the Margetts compound, but would not swear to this.

Margetts had a single rotary kiln and Peters a twin installation. The former was served by quite the largest factory chimney I saw in the South of England prior to the coming of the post-war generation of power stations, about the size of those at Dunstable and Rugby, if not quite as tall. Beside the footpath to Snodland Ferry was a lengthy disused part of this works. This included Margetts own cooperage which had been badly burned in a fire c.1911 — which my aunt had seen on her way home from the ferry and had raised the alarm — and never rebuilt. I found this a very eerie place all silent behind the corrugated iron fence — nothing would have induced me to walk to the ferry after dark, though it was once necessary to do so *from* there in company with my grandmother — I was terrified!

As a small boy, I remember being lifted on to the footplate of *Wouldham* one Sunday afternoon when she was brand new, I should think during the Winter of 1921. A few years later, I was told there were five locomotives and that 'the Compound' was too heavy for the track, so little used (this could only have been *Ninety Nine*). I never saw a traction engine type (2–2–0) being used. If there were indeed five engines at that time, one of them must have been *Victor*, though it seems unlikely. I do seem to remember being told that one engine was in pieces, so perhaps that was the one concerned. Thus, I only ever saw three engines, working or static, the two orthodox saddle-tanks and an Aveling & Porter locomotive with all wheels the same size, which again could only have been *Ninety Nine*. This engine was always used on the longish run to the upper level of the pit (perhaps this track was better laid, being on more permanent formation). This line still took the curious semi-circular route into the lower pit, rather than direct into one of the works. It passed on the far side of a field from the tip, on which my grandfather's house stood. On the far side of the line was an almost alpine area of waste, the origins of which always puzzled me, before coming to the steep descent into the main pit. This had increased in size very greatly since stretching towards Wouldham village, and nearly as far as the old Wouldham pit, situated just beyond what was known locally as the 'Lower Road'. The pit face was becoming progressively lower as the ground sloped away. I was told that the chalk from the upper level was used in the lime kilns, being better for this purpose. This pit was hand worked and loaded.

My grandfather was also responsible for wagon body repairs. The flap door at the lower end was a solid piece of oak. In September 1925, I was staying with my grandparents and was called from their garden by shouts of 'Train off line', so I went down into the lane and looked across the field. The eighth or ninth wagon of a train of some 27 had been derailed (I was told later by reason of a broken axle) and it had been smashed to pieces. Two or three other wagons were also off the road. The front part of the train went on with the crew (this engine was always manned by two men — I don't know about the others), and after an interval a gang appeared from the main pit, shovelled away the mound of chalk (it was still there years afterwards, gradually sinking lower and being coloured by moss) and barring the partly unloaded but relatively undamaged wagons back on the track, so that the rest of the train could proceed when the engine returned. It was my first sight of a railway accident; the first of many.

Peters and Margetts closed at Christmas 1925. Peters never reopened. Some of the lime kilns were worked subsequently, so that railway continued to be used a little, and then in 1928/9 (I think), Margetts reopened to make a 'continental' type of cement. The special ingredient arrived by barge (from France it was said) and trainloads of it were stored alongside the lime kilns. It had a reddish appearance and I have since assumed it was bauxite. Output was, I believe, small and had stopped before my grandfather moved away in 1931. It is doubtful whether production could have gone on much longer, even if economic, without starting an entirely new pit into the hillside proper behind Scarborough. There was a lot of talk locally about 'The Combine' only taking over the former owners so they could close down the works, and a good deal of feeling on the east bank of the Medway against William Lee Roberts, whose seemingly brash new works at Holborough was going great guns, at a time when the bigger works on the opposite side of the river was being closed down.'

The Lamb Inn Crossing, Greenhithe

Most works had level crossings over the streets, some 'flagged', some not. Only two gated crossings are recalled, and one of these was outside the Lamb Inn, where the double tracks from Johnson's Works to the Wharf crossed a by-road from Stone Crossing Halt to Greenhithe, running north of the railway. It was a busy crossing, because the electric transporters, which used the eastern track, were always on the move. There was not a lot of road traffic, though it was one way into the nearby Kent Works, and sometimes the gatekeeper would keep the gates shut for the road until something turned up. Just on the works side of the crossing, there were facing crossovers. As the tracks here were wide apart, to pass through the twin tunnels under the SR, it was possible to 'run round' 3 or 4 wagons here, and this was often done with main-line wagons brought down from the SR exchange siding. There was always something to see; the first sight of a Kent Works engine coming across was of special interest, as without exploring one did not know that the tangle of sidings at the riverside allowed through running between the two works.

Cotton Lane, Stone

One of the most interesting places on the North Kent cement lines was the junction just north of the tunnel under Cotton Lane, Stone. Originally there had been here only a line running under the SECR railway and the lane, from a large pit to the cement works in the Stone Court complex. However when the Kent Works was opened to the east in 1926, a spur line was run from the tunnel mouth through cutting and a skew bridge under the SR west of Stone Crossing Halt, to connect the pit with that works. Another line diverged between Cotton Lane and the SR to run in cutting to new pits to the west. By this time there were no cement works in the Stone Court area, though there was a whiting works, and some of the chalk from the western pits was being sent through to Kent Works. Though later the junction was relaid for through running from these pits to Kent Works, it was not so in the thirties. The mode of working was for a Stone Court engine to haul the filled train from the pit, reversing north of Cotton Lane and pushing the wagons into the tunnel; a Kent Works engine would emerge from its cutting and pick them up. In the other direction, the Kent Works engine would push the empties into the tunnel, the Stone Court engine would couple up, move towards the whiting works clear of the junctions, and then propel the train towards the face, turning right at the junction. The Stone Court trains comprised only 8–10 wagons, perhaps because the Falcon engines were light and old; the job of forwarding them to Kent Works usually fell to Kent Works engines *Toronto* or *Clarence*, while the heavier *Arthur* and *Stone* worked the long trains to the new pit south of Elizabeth Street (the east of Cotton Lane).

By means of the junctions described above, it would have been possible for an engine to run three miles from the furthest Stone workings to the furthest Johnson's workings; probably none ever did so, but an imaginary footplate trip may help to locate the various lines now difficult to trace. Leaving the furthest-west Stone Court pit, then being developed, one would go through a tight tunnel into a large pit being 'wound down', clatter through a passing loop, and through another tunnel into a rather smaller pit, then by yet another tunnel into a curving cutting now on the north side of Cotton Lane, to the junction near the whiting works; reverse into the tunnel, out again turning right, through a straight cutting under the SR, past the points leading to the exchange siding, then wander through the Kent Works complex taking every right-hand point that offered. We are now into the muddy area at the riverside, and, at an indeterminate point, on Johnson's Works metals. We carry on to join the right-hand of two lines passing over a gated crossing, and pass through the works to the right-hand of the main building; then comes a complex works junction, and we enter a tunnel 250 yards long, taking us under the London Road and a field. We come out into the deep curving 'Castle Pit' which is half a mile long; then comes a short tunnel under Hedge Place Road, another pit, and we cruise under a footpath bridge high above us into the southern-most pit, and the end of a journey, half of which has been up to 100 ft below ground level.

The Aveling & Porter engine *Ninety-nine* mentioned by Mr Lambert on a previous page, standing in the triangle at the 'Peters' engine shed, on the spur leading to 'Margetts'. This engine was built in 1899, 4 ft 3 in. gauge. R.G. Pratt

Appendix Two
Locomotives at Swanscombe Works

The following is part of the APCM Chief Engineer's report dated 27th February, 1918. It highlights the fact that then, as now, the boiler was the main problem in keeping engines on the road, and at this point in World War I it must have been specially difficult to foresee when major repairs could be done, due to the scarcity of fitters and materials:

Swanscombe Loco Boilers

It is understood that for the work in prospect, it will be necessary to keep ten locos running in general work, i.e. leaving out the upper clinker road and the uncallow*. For this, we have available seven large Aveling & Porter type, one special type — *Millbay* — now on siding work, and four Taylor type. This only allows for two to be under repair at one time, say one Aveling & Porter type and one Taylor type. It also necessitates taking *Millbay* off siding work.

AVELING & PORTER TYPE: Sundry repairs are required on these, but they are not of a very extensive nature and would not justify sending the locos off to the Works, although additional boilermakers might usefully be employed at Swanscombe.

TAYLOR TYPE: Of these four, the *Iron Horse* will be completely rebuilt at the end of the month, and *Chester* has recently had the firebox welded up and is satisfactory. The *Dead Horse* is now leaking but it should be got out again almost at once. As soon as *Iron Horse* is available it is proposed to endeavour to weld up all the leaky places in this box.

MILLBANK: This boiler is in very bad order and certain parts of the loco have been taken to complete the *Iron Horse*. It is proposed to fit a new boiler now in stock on this loco while the replacements are being made. The old boiler needs a new box for which enquiries are being made.

N.B.: The other two Taylor Type locos, namely the *Liverpool* and the *Swanscombe* both have their pressures reduced from 140 to 100 lb. and are in bad condition generally. It is proposed that these should be ultimately rebuilt similar to the other four.

---

* Thought to refer to the stripping of overburden: turf, earth, etc.

Appendix Three
Accidents

Collisions and derailments on the cement railways seldom had any serious consequences, as speeds were so low. It was still possible to get run over, especially in the tunnels. However, most accidents occurred during movements of wagons at the face, where it was slippery and loose chalk was often falling. The wagons may have looked like toys from the pit top, but down there if anyone was between them when they were shunted, or a sprag removed, the result could be serious injury. Some typical examples in Board of Trade reports have been abstracted below, by Mr Tom Burnham. The first name gives the identity of the pit, the second the responsible company. The Lamb pit is no doubt that south of the works but north of London Road, since this is not far from Lamb Terrace. The location of Old Estate and Downfield is not known.

These entries all relate to chalk quarries: there may have been accidents in clay pits, but most were less than 20 ft deep and not covered by the 1894 Quarries Act.

1896

A man named Charles Megan, 35 years of age, was run over by a locomotive while walking upon a railway leading from Clinkham Chalk Pit to the wharf on the banks of the Medway. Though not employed at the quarry, the man was perfectly well acquainted with the place; but as he was deaf and dumb, the accident is not surprising.

4th December, 1896
Lamb Cliff (Chalk). I.C. Johnson & Co. Ltd

William Crawford Sharp, 16, points shifter. In order to move the points, he jumped down from the locomotive on which he was riding, and was somehow run over by it. Killed on the spot.

24th October, 1898
Old Estate (Chalk). J. Bazley White & Brothers Ltd

Henry W. Simmens, 14, pointsboy. While he was standing between two wagons and coupling them together, the driver started the locomotive, not knowing that any coupling was going on. The deceased was caught between the buffers and died the same day.

23rd November, 1899
Downsfield (Chalk). J. Bazley White & Brothers Ltd

Arthur William Bignell, 18, pointsman. He was on night duty and somehow fell off the footplate of the locomotive, which passed over him before it could be stopped. Killed on the spot.

13th May, 1902
Northfleet (Chalk). APCM (1900) Ltd

Thomas Edgelar, 73, labourer. When leaving the quarry after the day's work by way of a tunnel through which the wagons of chalk are drawn by a locomotive, he was knocked down by the locomotive, and received such injuries that death resulted 40 hours afterwards.

18th December, 1902
Sharp's Green (Chalk). East Kent Chalk Quarry Co.

James Morgan, 30, platelayer. He put his foot on the buffer of a truck which was being shunted; losing his balance, he fell and was crushed between the truck and the side of the roadway.

11th August, 1902
Manor Works (Chalk). APCM (1900) Ltd

George Caller, 29, labourer. While engaged filling a tram or trolley-truck a large piece of chalk, 18 feet in length, fell upon him from the perpendicular side or face in consequence of an unseen 'back' or 'slip'.

17th November, 1902
West Kent (Chalk). West Kent PC Co.

Charles Beadle, 50, chalk digger. While he was loading a wagon, a piece of chalk fell from the face about 30 feet up, and rebounding from the loose chalk which he was filling into the wagon, struck him on the head and body. He died 3 days afterwards.

This typical World War I Baldwin engine, with its WD number 560 still just visible on the tank, was rebuilt by Bagnall before delivery in 1918 to the Rainham cement works 2 ft gauge railway. It saw little use and is seen here derelict in April 1934.

G. Alliez

Appendix Four

Survey of Chalk Pits

From 1922 to 1937 the Government maintained a register of pits more than 20 ft deep. The section covering the cement-producing districts of North Kent is useful in supplying in some cases names by which pits were known locally, ownership, and the period during which they were in use. It must be emphasised that the list is not exhaustive, not entirely reliable, and sometimes hard to interpret. The wording in brackets has been added by the present authors:

APCM

Alkerden clay-pit: 1922–37 (this was in fact a continuous deep wide trench).
Barnfield Whites: disused 1922, appears 1925–31 (probably the pit immediately west of Craylands Lane).
Borstal Manor: disused 1922.
Cliffe: disused 1922 (this would be the pit of Nine Elms Works).
Craylands, Swanscombe: 1922–37 (probably the pit in which the Crayland Siding was laid).
Frindsbury, Crown Works: disused 1922. Appears 1925–37.
Great Cluland, Bluebell Hill: 1922–8, also 1934–7. (Burham Works top pit, but the later date probably refers to the lower three-level pit.)
Halling Manor: disused 1922, appears 1925–37, not after (the bottom pit).
New Barn Swanscombe: disused 1922.[†]
Northfleet Chalk: disused 1922 (the one in which the paper works was built).
Southfleet Chalk: disused 1922. Appears 1928–37 (supplied London Works Northfleet).
Stone Chalk: 1922–37 (the pit that supplied Kent Works).
Histed Murston: 1922–28 (Smeed Dean); 1931–37 (APCM). (Should read Highsted; seems to have been out of use for three years before APCM acquired it).
London Portland Northfleet: 1928–37 (adjacent to Southfleet given above).
Swanscombe: 1928–37 (probably that south of Craylands).
Tolhurst Northfleet: 1931–37 (pit south of church re-worked by Whites).
Knockholt Barnfield Swanscombe: 1934 (should be Knockhall; large pit south of Knockhall House).
Lower Rainham: British Standard Cement[*] 1928: APCM 1931, not after.
Holborough: 1928 as Holborough Cement Co.; 1931–7 as APCM
Cliffe Clay: 1937 (the Alpha pit).
Stone Court Chalk: 1937 (probably the ones each side of the west end of Cotton Lane).
Western Cross Swanscombe: 1937 (the large pit south of Alkerden Lane).

BPCM

Lees Halling: 1922–37.
Red Lion Northfleet: disused 1922 (an unidentified old pit).
Stone Castle Greenhithe: 1922–5 (pit to west of Johnson's works).
Johnsons Greenhithe: 1928–37 (the long crescent shaped 'Castle Pit').
Town Wharf Greenhithe: 1922–5 (Globe Works pit).
New Globe Whiting Greenhithe: 1928. Disused 1931.

---

† There was an old pit west of Southfleet Road (610735) adjacent to New Barn; the large pit here east of Southfleet Road was probably dug after the survey ceased.

* British Standard Cement; this works was at Motney Hill; the pit cannot now be traced for certain, but may be that showing traces at Macklands.

Wickham: 1922–28. Disused 1931, appears again 1937 (the Martin Earle pit).
Beacons Wood Dartford Clay: 1937 (claypit for Johnsons).
Whorne's Place Strood: disused 1922 (Trechmann Weekes).
Wouldham Hall: 1922–31.

Gillingham Portland Cement, Court Field: 1922–37 (north-west of railway bridge at cemetery).

Alpha Cement Cliffe-at-Hoo: 1928–34, and 1937.
Alpha Cement Thames Works Clay: 1937.

Rugby Portland Cement Co. Ltd, Clinkham, Halling, white: 1931–4.
grey: 1931–4 (white pit was north of grey pit).

Note: some of the interpretations in brackets are tentative. The original list was kindly supplied by Mr T.G. Burnham.

After the clear-out of the Francis Works at Cliffe, one Aveling & Porter engine (2428) was left behind, and is here seen derelict in 1938. The ship's rigging block lying bottom right is a reminder that from here a sail-powered trolley was operating down to the river at the time. _R.W. Kidner_

Appendix Five

S.R. Sidings to Cement Works 1934

Name of siding	Position	Method of working
Murston PCM	Sittingbourne	Ground frame; Sykes' key from Sittingbourne Box
Wickham PCM	Down side, Cuxton–Strood	Wickham Siding Box
Weekes	Down side, Cuxton–Halling	Ground frame, out of use
Batchelors	Down side, Cuxton–Halling	Ground frame Sykes' lock and plunger from Cuxton Box
Hiltons	Down side, Halling	Halling Box
Lees	Down side, Halling–Snodland	Ground frame; electrical release Halling Box
Medway Works*	Up side, Snodland–Halling	Ground frame, electrical release Snodland Box
PCM	Up side, Snodland–Halling	Ground frame, electrical release Snodland Box
Stone Court	Down side Dartford–Stone crossing	Sykes' key from Dartford No. 2 Box
PCM	Down side, Stone Crossing–Greenhithe	Sykes' key from Dartford No. 2 Box
Johnson's	Up side, Stone Crossing–Greenhithe	From Stone Crossing Gatehouse Box
Ingress Park	Down side, Greenhithe–Northfleet (but connection from up line)	Ground frame, mechanical release from Greenhithe Box
Swanscombe	Down side, Greenhithe–Northfleet	Sykes' key from Greenhithe Box
Northfleet Deepwater	Down side, Northfleet	Hand points
PCM Strood	Strood	Hand points from No. 3 Siding
British Portland Cement	Gravesend West St	Hand points from Perry Street Siding

* This later became the north-end entrance to Holborough Works

Appendix Six

Aveling & Porter Locomotives

Aveling and Porter engines are very much part of the Kent cement works history. No other maker of steam geared locomotives turned out so many, until the popularity of 'Sentinels' in the twenties, and most of this output went to Kent, some 40 to cement manufacturers.

Thomas Aveling was a farmer from Ruckinge in Kent and was impressed by the need for a mechanical roller to improve the apalling roads in the county. He turned first to the engine, and designed a traction engine which was built by Clayton & Shuttleworth of Lincoln. He had a foundry in Rochester and made components to convert some 'portable engines' (owned by friends) into self-propelling engines. In 1861 he was able to build the first traction to be constructed in his own works. Almost at once an adaptation to rail use was produced: this speed may be due to the fact that Mr Porter was connected with the cement industry. Certainly by the mid-sixties Aveling had supplied a number of traction-engine-type locomotives to cement works in Essex and Kent. He did not solve the problem of casting and mounting a road roller until 1866, and thereafter road-rollers took most of the A&P production, with traction and rail engines as a minority interest.

The first rail engines, like the traction engines, were chain-driven; a heavy chain passed over a sprocket on a secondary shaft at the rear of the boiler and then over sprockets on both axles. His first design had 3 ft–4 ft wheels, a 5 ft 3 in. wheelbase and weighed 9 tons. That is for standard gauge; there was a smaller version for the narrow gauge with a wheelbase of less than 4 ft.

In the early seventies a change was made to gear drive, a large gear-wheel on the countershaft engaging with other large gears on one wheel or each axle. A different design was also offered, with large driving wheels on the rear axle only; between 1876 and 1899 all engines supplied to Kent cement firms were of this type, except for one, an unusual engine with four driving wheels and two high-pressure cylinders. This however was reconstructed from a locomotive supplied to the Brighton Tramways, which was returned as unsatisfactory. This pre-dated the first of the standard 0–4–0 type. From 1899 all four-wheels-driven engines were compound, though single-driven examples remained 'simple' with one cylinder. Single cylinder sizes ranged over the years between 8×10 ins and 11×12 ins; compound ones from $8\frac{7}{8} \times 14\frac{1}{2} \times 14$ ins to $10 \times 16\frac{1}{4} \times 14$ ins.

The first engines had no cabs; later ones had some protection, ending with an all-over cab covering, bunker, crankshaft and all — though oddly the last one built, in 1926, had no cab at all.

Two Aveling & Porter locomotives have been preserved. The 1926 'single' from Holborough went to the Bluebell Railway and at one time gave passenger trips (not very far!) The other is an 1872 chain-driven four-wheel-driven engine, one of a pair delivered to the Duke of Buckingham's Brill Tramway, which after later use in a brickworks at Weedon until 1940, is now in the care of London Transport.

One odd advantage of this type with the cylinders above the boiler was quoted by a driver from Wouldham Hall; when one was replaced by a Manning Wardle, its motion fouled the ground where the track had sunk!

Bibliography

For very many years industrial railways were never mentioned in railway literature; it is only in the last 20 years that articles and books have appeared in any number. Some other sources however can be found:

The Mining Journal from 1835 on
The Engineer from 1856 on
Engineering from 1866 on
The Locomotive Magazine 1896 on
The Blue Circle, published by APCM privately
The Industrial Railway Record
The Quarry
The Industrial Locomotive

The following articles should be noted:

The Swanscombe Cement Works Railway, The Locomotive 15th July, 1924
Aveling & Porter Engines, Engineering, 3rd August, 1866
Traction Engine Railway Locomotives, The Engineer, February 1957
Traction Engine Locomotives, Blue Circle Vol. 12, No. 3, July 1978
Frindsbury Cement Works, C. Down, IRS Record No. 16, December, 1967
Electric Bulk Cement Wagons (Johnsons) T.G. Burnham, Electric Railway Soc. Journal Jan./Feb. 1974
'An Electric Quarry Line in Derbyshire and Kent', T.G. Burnham, Electric Railway Soc. Journal Sept./Oct. 1978

Two books which are of great interest though dealing only marginally with the railways are:

The Cement Industry 1796–1914, A.J. Francis, David & Charles 1977
Industrial Medway, J.M. Preston, privately 1977

Some early history can be found in Limes, Calcareous Cements and Mortars by Colonel Pasley, published 1838.
Traction Engine Locomotives, Ian K. Hutchinson, Road Locomotive Society 1981: useful for detailed lists of Aveling & Porter locomotives.
The History of Blue Circle, Peter Pugh, Cambridge Business Publishing, 1988: useful for the period after 1914.